I HAVE MET HIM

André Frossard

I HAVE MET
HIM

God Exists

Translated by
MARJORIE VILLIERS

HERDER AND HERDER

1971
HERDER AND HERDER NEW YORK
232 Madison Avenue, New York 10016

Original edition: *Dieu existe, je L'ai recontré* © 1969, by Libraire Arthème Fayard, Paris.

Library of Congress Catalog Card Number: 72-147031

English translation © 1970, by William Collins Sons & Co. Ltd.

Printed in Great Britain

TO MY PARENTS

The translator would like to thank Professor John Reid for his kindness in reading the English text and improving it.

If some of the branches were broken off and you, a wild olive shoot, were grafted in their place to share the richness of the olive tree, do not boast over the branches. If you do boast, remember it is not you that support the root, but the root that supports you.

You will say, 'Branches were broken off so that I might be grafted in.' That is true. They were broken off because of their unbelief, but you stand fast only through faith. So do not become proud, but stand in awe. For if God did not spare the natural branches, neither will he spare you.

ST PAUL

'CONVERTS are embarrassing,' said Bernanos.

For this reason, as well as others, I have waited a long time before writing this book. It is difficult to describe one's own conversion without writing about oneself, and it is still more difficult to write about oneself without being complacent or writing ironically and thereby, in a crafty manner, attributing to oneself a few more faults than one has and so disturbing the reader's judgment.

None of this would matter but for the fact that the evidence stands or falls with the witness and there is therefore a danger that if the one is rejected the other will be too.

In the end, I became convinced that a witness, however unworthy, who happens to know the truth, owes it to himself to speak out, hoping that the evidence, because of its intrinsic merit, will gain a credence which the witness himself would not deserve on his own account.

Thanks to an extraordinary event I know the truth about the world's most controversial problem and hold the answer to its age-old question.

God exists.

I have met him.

*

I met him accidentally, by chance – usually there seems to be an element of chance in this sort of occurrence.

I was amazed, as astonished as I should have been had I turned the corner of a Paris street and instead of seeing the familiar cross-roads found myself faced by a limitless sea washing the foundations of the houses and spreading away into infinity. That moment of stupefaction is still with me. I have never got used to the existence of God.

*

At 5.10 p.m. I entered a chapel in the Latin Quarter in search of a friend; I came out at 5.15 p.m., having been taken into a friendship which is not of this world.

I went in as a sceptic, as an atheist holding extreme left-wing views. My mind was full of other things; more than this, I was quite uninterested in a God whom I no longer even thought of denying, believing that for a long time the question of God's existence had been relegated to the profit and loss account of human fear and ignorance. A few minutes later I emerged 'Catholic, Apostolic, Roman', carried forward on an immense wave of joy.

When I went in I was twenty years old; when I came out I was a wide-eyed child ready to be baptized and gazing with wonder at a heaven that was peopled, at this town which did not realize that it was suspended between heaven and earth, at these human beings on whom the sun shone but who seemed to walk in darkness unaware of the great tear that had just appeared in the world's canvas.

My reactions, the landscape of my mind, my intellectual scaffolding, all these things, by which I had lived cosily, had vanished; my habits too were gone, and my tastes had changed.

*

I am not unaware that a conversion of this kind by its very unpremeditatedness will shock many of my contemporaries and will strike them as totally unacceptable for they prefer rational approaches to mystical thunderclaps and more and more they have come to dislike divine intervention in daily life.

Yet, however much it might please me to fall in with the mood of this age, I cannot describe slow stages of development, when, in truth, there was a sudden change, nor can I reveal the recent or remote psychological causes of this change, because no such factors came into it. I cannot describe the path by which I reached faith, because I was on a different road and I was thinking about quite other things when I fell into what I can only call an ambush.

This book does not tell how I became a Catholic but how, when I was not going towards Catholicism, I found myself to be a Catholic.

It is not an account of an intellectual development, but the record of a fortuitous event, something akin to an investigation of an accident.

If I have found it necessary to describe my childhood at some length this is not to draw attention to my background but to establish the fact that nothing in my past led up to what happened to me.

Divine charity itself has its *actes gratuits*. If I am often obliged to talk in the first person, this is because it is clear to me, as it will I hope soon be to you, that I played no part in my own conversion.

But it is no use saying such things; I must prove them, and so, here are the facts.

My father's village was the only one in France where there was a synagogue but no church.

It is near Belfort, surrounded by a countryside of turf and mist, one of those eastern regions which are slow to welcome the sun and behind whose coverts the pale ghosts of invading armies are always on the march. The houses cling to the slopes to withstand the wind and pull down their tile bonnets, Alsatian fashion, till they nearly cover their eyes.

At long intervals grey loaf-shaped stones stick out of the clay. Some are mere stumps showing where the old German frontier ran, others mark a soldier's grave: here lies an Austrian officer, his head-piece sealed with granite, there, Pegoud, pilot, a dragonfly smashed after a short descent in flaming glory and now frozen into rigidity at the edge of this little wood.

Foussemagne: four hundred inhabitants, set against an horizon barred by the black spears of pine trees, in an arena of clay and containing one tile factory whose chimneys of varying heights provide the seasonal rendez-vous of storks and strike two red lines across a faded Breughel canvas.

*

Attracted by the liberal outlook of the local land-owners, the Comtes de Reinach-Foussemagne, a fairly

12

large colony of Jews settled in the village in medieval times.

Hence the pink granite synagogue not far from the Town Hall, a huge building of unidentifiable style whose walls are pierced by the kind of windows usually to be found on the staircase of a middle-class residence.

Except on great feasts the synagogue was not much frequented but it was always haunted by the shabby silhouette of the rabbi. Poor and discreet, he had married late in life a woman older than himself. The pair made one think of two humble sparrows perching on a seven-branched candlestick. Their meek chirps and obvious destitution caused their co-religionists to remark with affectionate sympathy: 'To be a rabbi is no career for a Jew.'

Were ours practising Jews? Their religion seemed to us to be based more on keeping the law and the rules of morality than on pious exercises. They were bound to certain observances and these they fulfilled: the keeping of Saturday as the day of rest, the laws of Moses concerning fasting and the preparation of food. Faithfully they celebrated the Passover, a mysterious feast whose ceremonies included the making of unleavened bread, wonderfully white with little bubbles that the warmth of the oven had slightly browned. Once a year they came to the synagogue, with a sheepskin flung across their shoulders, to prepare with a night of prayer for the fast of Yom Kippur. Sometimes on the following day a hungry fellow would drop in at our house, rather furtively, and with some amusement we would watch him vaguely pluck a raisin or two or munch a piece of sugar, all the while talking brightly about the weather

13

and the crops. Were they believers? Surely. It is one and the same thing to be a Jew and to be a believer; a Jew cannot deny his God without denying himself. But they never said a word about religion to us, for we were amongst the most notorious of Red republicans.

The two communities lived side by side without quarrelling and so had no need to build defences. As a child I spent most of my holidays in this curiously assorted village without knowing that there were people who believed there was a Jewish problem.

The Christians had their feasts, they went off to other villages, where there were churches, to celebrate them; the Jews had their feasts and these were on different dates. The Christians had their day of rest on Sunday and the Jews had theirs on Saturday, which was convenient since it provided everyone with an early example of the 'English weekend'.

The Christians had their cemetery and the Jews had one near Belfort; my grandmother was buried in it and that was all I knew.

*

The frontiers between minds did not pass through the area of religion but through that of politics. There were 'Blacks' considered by the 'Reds' to be monstrous survivors of a past age. Black they were as the suits they wore for weddings and funerals, black as the cassocks of their priests, black as the primeval darkness in which they had been bred. The Blacks voted for the possessors, even though most of them were as poor as the rest of us. Respectful of the established order of things, they did not wish it to be changed, not even to improve it. To us they seemed to be mainly concerned with obeying and with showing respect.

The leader of the Reds was my grandfather, a leather-worker by trade, who proclaimed himself a radical republican. In those days, when socialism had not yet reached the village, one could not declare more categorically that one was a revolutionary.

In the evenings the men from the tile factory and the republican peasants would meet in his workshop and talk politics while he went on cutting and sewing by the light of his lamp. Talking politics meant talking about destitution. In those days workmen were paid five to ten sous a day and they were envied by the peasants whose miserly strips of earth scarcely provided them with enough to eat.

No law protected the factory hand who could not escape from his poverty even by working ten or twelve hours a day; as for the peasant, he was entirely at the mercy of the vagaries of the weather and could not expect help from anyone.

This was *La Belle Époque*. The lord of the manor was no longer the Comte de Reinach-Foussemagne; his estates had long ago been broken up and sold. The owner of the tile factory had taken his place. He lived near his works, in a big, rather ugly, red brick house which we children thought as grand and luxurious as Versailles must be. It was filled in our imagination with huge toys and within it were lights and laughter and no one who lived there was ever unhappy. Yet, cheeky as we normally were, we never dared go too close to the house and we were scared by the pointed tips of the railings which surrounded it. It might be the place of happiness, but it

15

shopkeeper criticized, blamed and advised the other players. He was one of those who took even more interest in his partner's cards than in his own. While he was gravely lecturing a bored audience, my uncle would roll a cigarette of greyish tobacco, slipping the edge of the paper beneath his executive moustache to lick it, then place the finished article behind his right ear as though it were a clerk's pencil and put an end to the harangue by dealing a new hand.

Under its garlanded china shade, the forty-watt lamp shone remorselessly on the players, the bench, the bits of leather, the tangle of reins, the empty ovals of the harness collars, on all these familiar people and things which electric light had deprived of something extra, something amusing, that was in fact the shadow they used to cast when the room had been lit by a paraffin lamp.

We children (I had two cousins of my own age) watched the card-players with varying degrees of interest. The youngest boy, who looked like a pretty little girl, soon went back to the kitchen, the elder boy stuck it out for longer; finally we all went up to our arctic bedrooms where there was sometimes ice in our water jug. I slipped quickly between the sheets of my bed which seemed all the heavier for the huge eiderdown that was puffed up like a great *beignet* of feathers, masking nearly all the room and half the ceiling from my view.

When I was at last all alone in the darkness I felt very safe. It was true that I couldn't see a thing but then equally no one could see me.

When I had turned out the light I was sometimes attracted to the strange world on the other side of the window. This was not the start of a nightmare but the beginning of an adventure. I took advantage of the nightly return of infinity to escape from the now undefined shape of things. I seemed to be wandering somewhere between the earth and the moon, my senses very much on the alert, trying to penetrate some secret, trying to overhear some communication between a blade of grass and a nebula. I was sure that these worlds, so mysteriously connected, and surely in collusion, would some day drop one word too many – the one that would give me the clue to the riddle.

I was advancing in silence towards some imminent truth and just as I was about to discover what it was sleep always rubbed away the picture which the night had been creating with its symbols.

WINTER was more fun than summer. When work in the fields was over, darkness and cold brought us early to the fireside and endowed the snow-covered house with a sense of inner life compounded of the smell of wet logs and good soup which reached us as we sat round the cast-iron stove, stretching our numb hands out to it, lost in vague thoughts.

This was also the season of a strange assemblage of feast days. There was that of St Nicholas, who was called Santa Claus at the top of the village, the part that lies near the old frontier. Santa Claus personified paternal justice, he rewarded the good and punished the bad (but we didn't have any bad children in our village). He was a popular character on calendars and postcards, and the frost on his cloak always left a few bits of glitter on our fingers.

On Christmas Eve, long after dark, the 'Blacks', wearing their Sunday best, went off to their mummings (as we called them, without any malice). They carried lanterns, talked louder than usual and seemed very happy.

We understood them no better than we understood the attachment of the Jews to their religious exercises. It seemed to us that both wasted a lot of time singing for no good reason.

Next day the church bells of the neighbouring villages

laid a ceremonial veil over the dead countryside. No echo greeted them from our churchless village.

We too put on our smart suits – to go nowhere.

Our uncle gave us presents he had made himself, pretty little whips with white leather lashes, belts and satchels of green stuff lined with leather. When we ran to school with the satchels slung over our backs we must have looked like small infantrymen pursuing learning as she fled before us.

Our aunt, a robust but gently mocking Alsatian woman, stuffed one cake after another into the white-hot oven. We ate in the largest of our rooms (it was usually closed) on the white table-cloth which we kept for great occasions.

But not even the Alsatian wine, nor the beer nor the raspberry syrup succeeded in making our family talkative. Neither the meal, much richer than our usual fare, nor the fir-tree with its silver garlands commemorated any event. It was a Christmas lacking any religious context, a Christmas that had lost its memory; it was not anyone's feast.

GOD did not exist. His image, the images which remind
one of his existence and of the existence of what one
might call his descendants in time, the saints, the pro-
phets, the heroes of the Bible, were not to be seen in our
house.

He was never mentioned.

The Jews did not tell us anything about their religion.
They are not propagandists, for their religion is a family
affair, and they do not regard it as being of any interest
to strangers, even if these should happen to be half
Jewish.

In the event, our disinterest in religion made us tolerant
and this was a kind of insurance as far as the Jews were
concerned. While we were leftists because of our atheism,
they voted left so that they might be able to remain
peacefully pious, if pious they were – and if they shared
our views it was the better to preserve their own. They
lived the mysterious life of a community that had been
dispersed for two thousand years and yet had remained
homogeneous, sprinkled among the nations like yeast
(which the heavy German dough was before very long
to try to suffocate once and for all); unchanging and yet
peculiarly gifted for adaptation, they were faithful even
in unbelief – indeed some of those who asserted that
they were non-believers were even more pernickety than

the believers about the laws and injunctions of the Old Testament. Able to stand up to any defeat and also, which is rarer, to any success, they were able to understand everything; everything, that is, except what a Jew is. But who can answer that question?

As for the Christians of our village, they told us nothing about being a Christian. Perhaps this was out of discretion, or perhaps in order to avoid our sarcastic remarks. The results of their piety were not visible to the naked eye. Except for the increase in pastry-making that accompanied the bell-ringing feasts we had no idea what these days meant to them.

The moral standards of the Christians seemed much the same as ours. True they practised one or two specific virtues, such as obedience and humility, which appeared to us to be grave faults; besides this their behaviour seemed to be governed by a belief in future reward and a fear of future punishment which suggested a mercenary outlook of which we took a poor view.

They did not know, as we had known since the time of Jean Jacques Rousseau, that original sin had been abolished by the edict of a philosopher and that man was naturally good.

They seemed to hold that man was naturally bad. The Christians of those days had yet to discover nature, the possibilities of science and the benefits of freedom. They moved around cautiously between prohibitions, they dared not investigate things and they skimmed over the question of creation. They gave us the impression that they were frightened of life, terrified of abusing their capacity for living.

There remained nature which, given its pseudonym

'creation', might have suggested the idea of a creator. But the inexorable law which pushes the little fish into the jaws of the big fish and the antelope between the paws of the lion did not seem to suggest that nature practised the precepts of the Gospel; besides, the fact that Catholics seemed to regard nature with suspicion caused us to harbour fraternal feelings for it. Nature has no faith and that made her our ally against the believers. If the believers had their revelations (something I was to learn about later), nature with its great field of experience and scientific discoveries was our source of knowledge. Ourselves a part of nature, obliged to suffer the same risks and to endure the same inequalities, it was we who would redeem her and who would one day moderate her excesses and cause her laws to become more humane. If we had known that there was a God, nature by drawing us to herself would have separated us from him.

But as I have said, there was no God. Heaven was empty and the earth a combination of chemical elements arranged in fantastic patterns by the natural forces of attraction and repulsion. Soon she would communicate her deepest and last secrets to us, among them the fact that there was no God.

We were what could be called perfect atheists, the kind that no longer ever question their atheism. The militant anti-clericals who still survived and spent their time speaking at public meetings against religion seemed to us rather touching and rather ridiculous, as might an historian intent on debunking the tale of Little Red Ridinghood.

Their misguided zeal was merely uselessly prolonging

an argument to which reason had long ago provided the answer. For by this time the perfect atheist was no longer the one who denied the existence of God but the one for whom the question of God's existence did not arise.

THE annual fair, which caused the muddy grass of the recreation ground to be covered by planks, which brought out paper garlands, a few booths and a band to play for the dance, competed with politics as the main source of village entertainment. Election campaigns seemed to thaw out the left-wing families and bring a little life to them. In right-wing households politics were considered a vice, improbably sanctioned by the hierarchy but about which, all the same, it was better not to speak in front of the children.

On Sundays the men disappeared and returned very late from the neighbouring villages, foot-weary and boasting and, for once, in high spirits and loquacious about the way in which they had dealt with their adversaries.

The right-wing candidates were interviewed at the Town Hall in the recreation room, where no recreations ever took place except for those unintentionally provided by these characters, whom all supporters of the Left felt obliged to silence.

My uncle and his neighbour the smith took a certain malicious delight in attending these meetings wearing their holland or leather aprons, thereby drawing the attention of the intruder to the fact that the hard conditions in which the workers lived did not allow them time to change before a meeting and that they had been obliged to come between two strokes of the hammer, taking the time off their dinner-break. Of course they did not come to hear what the candidate had to say but only to repel the attack of the forces of reaction. Their means of doing so were not always gentle.

The most surprising candidate I saw subjected to the hostility of this inhospitable village was Tardieu, an important statesman of the Third Republic and, when allowed to open his mouth, a talented orator. He leaned against an iron pillar, surrounded by roaring left-wingers who had corralled his supporters into another part of the room and who were hurling curses at him. Silent of necessity and smiling out of bravado, he stood there un-ruffled, playing with a long cigarette-holder which some-how made him look like an amused St Sebastian engaged in smoking his arrows. After half an hour he left; though followed by the howls of his audience, he was intact and satisfied. Certainly he had not been able to say a word but he had imposed his presence, and no right-wing candidate could hope to do more than that in Fousse-magne.

Left-wing candidates rarely went to the Town Hall, preferring the café with its rowdy atmosphere and its clouds of smoke, which seemed to symbolize both factory work and the trail of forward-going thought. The right-wingers did not attempt to prevent their opponents from talking for they were already on the defensive. The future did not belong to them; the Right stood for tradition, for the cult of ancestors and for the past, areas which the Left had abandoned to it without a fight before forbid-ding the right-wingers ever to leave them.

When the election was over (as a rule the Left lost),

life returned to its orderly course, governed once more by the local virtues, the most noticeable of which was fidelity.

The fidelity of the people of eastern France is as inalienable a quality as being born fair or dark. In the first place they are faithful to their countryside, which seems to them to have a charm that is quite invisible to strangers, who are, as a rule, in a great hurry to leave this draughty cross-road celebrated only for the invasions it has known.

Who said that love is blind? Only love has good sight and is able to perceive beauty where those lacking love see nothing at all. Moreover, the glance of love is always also the glance of astonishment. This is true of the inhabitant of Belfort. When he looks at his flat countryside, with its few shrubs bending over the flooding river, he tastes all the joys of nature and comes very near to relaxing the tight hold he usually exerts upon his feelings. (But in fact he manages to avoid this weakness.)

The huge lion carved by Bartholdi in the grey granite of these fortifications, which have three times withstood a German attack, is his ancestor. He has developed the outlook of someone in a perpetually besieged city. His town is impregnable, and so is he.

Faithful to his land, just because it is so exposed to attack, he is faithful also to his family, to his friends, to his calling and to his house. His habits become rites and all the things which make up his life turn into institutions. To move to another place is a very serious matter, while to change one's opinion is a military defeat. In the revolutionary milieu in which I was brought up we had very serious thoughts about changing the world but we would never have dreamed of moving a clock from one place to another.

When, after the war, it was decided to rebuild the house which had been destroyed by a small bomb (it had had no difficulty in dealing with the old beams and thatch), my uncle was adamant that it must be restored complete with all its age-old inconveniences. He would certainly have been very unhappy if we had made any improvements, for this would have made him feel as though he was moving house, something almost unheard of and equivalent to deserting one's post.

Intellectually, morally and, so far as is possible, physically, the frontier-dweller does not change garrison.

His seeming inflexibility is really a solid attachment to all that fate has bestowed on him. One can understand why he is not very expansive with others when one realizes that he has to be so terribly firm with himself.

Like most of my compatriots I don't doubt that to my dying day I should have retained the ideas of my youth had not these been, as you will see, brutally contradicted by incontrovertible evidence.

WHILE our parents were fighting reaction, we children were finishing the siege of Troy. At the age of nine, among the few books in our house that were not about politics, I discovered the *Iliad* and I lived in it for years. It was a magic book, made of ivory and blue mosaic, in which the same words developed a curious luminous quality by being constantly repeated in the land of poetry.

For years I tried to understand the secret of those works which still remain fresh though they were written centuries ago. Eventually I noticed, long after everyone else had done so, that they were not affected by time, simply because time does not enter into them. Time is absent from the *Iliad*, or to be more accurate, it is reduced to the status of thought's slave. Between the moment at which the javelin leaves the hero's hand and that at which it pierces his adversary, there has been time for a speech, a reply, a meeting of the minor gods and arbitration by the Olympians. Poetry controls the movements of the heavenly bodies and the sun does not set until it has nothing further to look at on the earth.

My youthful atheism was in no way upset by the intrusions of the Olympians. On the contrary, everything they did was so natural that there was nothing supernatural left about them. The obstinacy with which they tried to conquer ordinary human beings had something

making shop with its lasts, some with pointed prows that reminded one of gondolas, these for the fashionables, and some with prows like those of barges, these for the able seamen, and, as well, lots of curled shavings of white-wood. Then there was a huge millstone for pressing cider apples. This stood under a lime-tree which rose to a great height and had been a Liberty Tree. (Limes do not fill me with enthusiasm and can there be anything in the world less free than a tree?)

Most of the villagers belonged to a sect called the Pietists. There were also a number of Lutherans and a few people who were neither the one nor the other, who seemed uninterested in religion and whom both the Pietists and the Lutherans referred to as 'pagans'.

The Pietists had neither clergy nor sacraments; on Sundays any member of the congregation who felt inspired to officiate said the prayers and read the Scriptures to the assembly which gathered in a barn or shed.

These Pietists, who are so prompt with their quotations and so used to being unpopular because of their exceptionally strict way of life, remind one of the Puritan in a Western film, who quotes the Bible and always opposes the hero, who is continually in a hurry, delaying him with sayings that, though irrelevant, appear to close the argument. Our villagers were always happy to voice biblical allusions in counterpoint. They had a preference for the Old Testament, which is the testament of the strong; their wives were often named Ruth or Esther.

When one investigated the history of their religion one realized that it had once been in contact with the Gospels but that its roots went back to the beginning of time via a

35

sinful world which the Pietists' taste for historical parallels peopled with Midianites and Philistines.

The Lutherans did not like the Pietists, partly because there were many more of them and partly because they gave the Lutherans the disagreeable feeling that they themselves were only partly reformed.

IF at Foussemagne no one was rich, at Colombier-Châtelot everyone was poor. Poverty had obliged my grandparents to leave the square house by the riverside. Now they lived in two rooms on the first floor of a semi-detached house, one of a row of cob-walled cottages. On the ground floor, which was tiled but was always damp, lived an old aunt so well wrapped up in rags that all one ever saw of her was the end of her nose or her finger-tips. She lived on water, the few vegetables that grew in her patch and the crumbs that fell from the first floor.

A rickety staircase, as steep as a ladder, led up to our living-room. Here was a stove which burned wood and a stone sink without a hot or a cold tap, a table covered with scabby linoleum and a glass-fronted dresser, which I never had any temptation to investigate knowing that its vast hold contained only a meagre cargo of herbs.

We slept in the other room, my grandfather in a bunk from which he slid down in the mornings to perform the physical jerks which were a vestige of his life as a police-man, bends, torso-testing and savate blows, all of which helped him to retain the bearing of a young man. My grandmother slept under the steps which led to the loft and I at her feet, on a good wool mattress.

Of course, I was the last to get up but it seemed to me that it was still very early in the morning when I heard the mowers rattling their reapers in the next-door yard – we did not have any expensive mechanical gadgets in those days – the slap of the reins as they were put through the rings of the harness and the whinnying of the horse as he tried ineffectually to free himself from the shafts. I ran to the kitchen to drink a bowl of milk and then to the stream to give myself a cat's lick, after which I came back, sat by the window and looked out at the day.

Towards ten o'clock my grandmother put a few provisions into a bag and we went off to join my grandfather in the fields. As he had no reaper he had to work earlier and later than the other men. After a walk along dusty little paths we guessed where he was when we heard the rasp of the scythe on the whetstone. Soon afterwards we saw him in the golden trench of a wheat-field or among scattered heaps of weeds. We put our dinner safely in the shade of a tree or by some spring and then we came back to do our share of the work. I was not able to tackle the wheat which was heavy and needed to be handled forcefully but also carefully so that the grain was not lost; but I was good for the minor task of haymaking. Over and over again in the buzzing heat I turned the grass, made it into stooks and finally placed these on a cart pulled by a poor fly-ridden horse which it was one of my tasks to encourage with a hazelnut switch.

My grandfather had made me tools suited to my years: a rake with only one set of teeth (to reduce by half the risk of hurting myself should I fall on it) and a little fork, its wooden points carefully blunted, so that I could occupy myself with trying to be useful. To tell the truth I detested my work in the fields, even though the part I played was so small. The fields were too large, the sky too merciless, the horse too big.

The best moment of the day was when we unpacked our lunch in some shady spot and laid out the slab of cheese wrapped in a wet cloth with a red border, and the bread, which was soggy on the side which had touched the bottle of lemonade laced with wine. But even this short cool respite was spoilt by the prospect of the return home, the knowledge that we should have to sweat in the dust as we heaved great armfuls of hay into the loft.

My taste ran not to earth, but to water; water that was transparent, free, devoid of memory and, according to Homer, brought no return.

My grandfather said he was a socialist, a profession of faith which can't have helped him in his career in the police force. He was seen at the chapel only when there was a funeral. He never mentioned religion, not even to be sarcastic about priests (anyhow they were an unknown species in the area). The pastor sometimes visited the village but I do not think that even curiosity ever caused him to cross the threshold of our house; therefore, since I did not attend funerals, I hadn't any idea what this man, always clothed in black, did; all I knew was that he was regarded with respect by the Lutherans and that the Pietists were suspicious of him.

If my grandfather had no religion he was not short of ethics; indeed, he seemed to have a surplus of morality which he showered on those not so favoured. He was born a righter of wrongs and in all the village quarrels he supported the cause of justice. His crusades brought him enemies as well as friends. He communicated with the wrong-doers by way of posters on which he inscribed in large letters remarks such as 'Pray less and stop stealing'. These he set up at the edge of his holding, overlooking the road. The neighbours did not hold his narrowness against him. For one thing he knew about plants and was good at treating nasty wounds and they often came to him for help while waiting for the bearded and devoted local doctor who usually couldn't be found.

There was an old apothecary's cabinet in our room; it was filled with dried herbs, powders in small boxes and sachets, all carefully labelled. I was forbidden to touch them but I had no wish to do so. I had my toys, made for me, made before my eyes in the workshop where the planks were stacked and the tools that needed mending were kept. Not all children have the fun of seeing the present they are going to be given actually take shape before their eyes, as it is whittled away by their grandfather whose hands, having just dropped the spade, have been turned into those of a magician. (Since then I have understood why in fairy stories the magician is often an old man.)

Besides these I had whistles made of elder, bows made of hazel, arrows made of willow and a sort of syringe with which to keep the dogs off our lettuce patch, and at the end of the year I was given two or three pence with which to buy sticks of liquorice.

My Grandmother Schwob allocated half a napoleon to her grandchildren each year. My grandfather couldn't keep up that style but he gave us his pence in a box which had held cough lozenges and this, in our eyes, added enormously to the value of his present. He always chose sliding boxes on which I could not hurt myself. Today I wonder whether he bought the lozenges for his cough or for the box.

Sunday was the Lord's Day for the Lutherans who sometimes went to the chapel, which was a few kilometres away, and also for the Pietists, who went in little groups to their meeting under the uncomprehending gaze of the Philistines.

For us it was the day when we had a proper bath in the

trout-stream, after which my grandfather rubbed my head with a concoction made up of camomile and rum, and twisted the long curls I wore for some time into corkscrews.

My mother's youngest brother, who lived with us, used to take me fishing, a sport which he pursued in defiance of the bye-laws. This adventurous, passionate young man had all the gifts I most envied: strength, daring, skill at all violent games and the sort of hirsute good looks that one is apt to attribute to Heathcliff in *Wuthering Heights*.

My mother had had another brother, fair, fragile and a musician, whose gentleness offset the alarm with which she regarded the reckless unruliness of the other. The musician died young 'of chest trouble'. I do not now know whether I ever saw him or whether the memory I have of a kind of angel violinist who arrived one night in the farm-yard and was gone long before dawn is really of him or only based on the stories I heard of his charm and his misfortunes.

He was handsome, as were all the others on that side of my family, all, except myself. I was not pleased with my face when I contemplated its dim reflection in the windows or in the blades of the kitchen knives, though these last were apt to reflect only my nose.

MY grandmother, whose face, beneath a cloud of white hair, was tiny and fine-drawn made me think of a bird which has been picked up by a well-intentioned but rough policeman.

She sang all day, in her kitchen, in the loft, by the stream as she washed her linen, in the field as she handled her rake, in the woods as she picked blackberries or chestnuts. The songs she sang were ballads of *La Belle Époque* in which knights of the moonlight waltzed with their lady-loves to melancholy music. Life with her was a mournful operetta, staged without any hope of an audience, with shabby scenery and sung by a fragile overworked Cinderella who was never destined to see her grey frock turn into a court gown or her pumpkin changed into a coach.

In the evenings she would take me on her knees and sing me a lullaby which went: 'Over there, over there, over there, there, there . . .' Although the song seemed to have no other words, it nevertheless lasted for a good quarter of an hour; yet it made me smile and sleep and dream. Probably I owe it to my grandmother that I can stand up better than some to liturgical litanies which people are apt to consider overlong, whereas I find them too short.

Once a week, during the summer, she went to the market to sell her vegetables. Very early in the morning

I used to see her start off on the path along the gulley which led to the local town. She was hardly taller than the palings which bordered the gardens she passed as she pushed her barrow loaded with beans and peas and carrots, avoiding a puddle here or a stone there.

In the afternoon she came home with a few pence, took off her muddy boots, put on her clogs and went back to her humble tasks: the beasts to care for, the men to feed, the housework to do, her grandson to rock, and the ritual of the end of the day, the closing of the doors of the stable, the barn, and the house and that of her own room to which she retired after everyone else had gone to bed and she had put out the lamp.

She gave me biscuits and kissed me, good smacking peasant kisses that sounded like the popping of champagne corks; I never saw her in a temper or even cross. Whatever annoyed her or made her sad she worked off in her songs. She was gentleness, tenderness and total resignation personified, she embodied those shades of feeling which, when there is no more to be said, can still be expressed in music.

She didn't walk, she trotted without pause, from the stove to the sink, to throw grain to the hens or pushing her barrow. Her movements were those of a well-wound-up mechanical toy, she was untiring, or so at least we thought who never saw her seated except leaning forward with her feet under the seat of her chair, ready to be off at any moment. She was not very old when she died of pernicious anaemia, which now bears another name but is still as fatal. She had been moved to the Protestant hospital in Besançon, where I went with my mother to visit her. The last time we were there it seemed to me that

44

the town with its fine façades, which for us were the most opulent buildings in the whole world, was damp and empty. The nuns, knowing how gravely ill she was, had moved her into a large room with tall curtainless windows that opened on to a garden. She was white under her white hair and more fine-drawn than ever, and she seemed to be screwed up in the middle of the bed as though she dared not occupy the whole of it. She was in no way rebellious but as pleasantly welcoming as usual, just a little more remote and very surprised to be served by 'educated ladies', who occasionally opened the door and then quietly went away when they realized that she had no requests to make. She was no more concerned with herself than ever she had been and her last words were words of pity for the suffering of another.

Her eyes that were now too weak to read were often turned towards a crucifix which hung on the wall in front of her bed. On the day she died she looked at it for a long time and said, in a tone of gentle compassion:

'The poor man.'

LIVING with these two old people – they may not after all have been as old as all that – who were determined to return me to my family at the end of the holidays contented and knowledgeable about country things, I was a happy child in a fairly unhappy village.

Colombier-Châtelot's inhabitants did not form a 'consumer society'. Indeed, it would have been more accurate to describe them as a 'non-consumer' society, since their efforts were directed to borrowing as little as possible of the goods of this world and to being content with little or nothing.

The low return on a holding that had been divided and subdivided till it no longer provided a living for anyone forced all the peasants to adopt a second means of livelihood. One was a carpenter, another the undertaker. A few, but they were getting scarce, mended watches by their window-sills during the hours of full daylight. It was touching to see those thick, cracked peasant fingers patiently engaged in persuading the tiny cogs to tick in concert within their metal shell.

Many families sent their girls and boys to work at the chair-making workshop in the neighbouring village or to the big factory in the town, whose buses scoured the whole area every morning collecting work-hands.

But even the addition of the children's wages could not lift the family out of poverty.

Most houses had an earth floor and if the barn had planks that was merely to prevent heavy hay-wains from making ruts. The people asked no more of life than the most common of its gifts and many things that are normally considered necessities were regarded by them as superfluous. Their existence was an endless succession of daily tasks, mostly seasonal and recurrent, which no one had any way of escaping or would have dreamed of shirking. Temptation took the traditional form of the boundary stone that jumps out of its hole by night to go and plant itself a little further along with the result that fields were apt to have a variable area. If the peasants had other temptations no one was allowed to guess what they might be.

The Pietists announced that they were the elect and were made both proud and patient by the fact. Our views concerning 'election' were very different; we regarded election as a process which was conducted from the bottom up and not something which came down from on high. Our agnostic ethics based on reason led us only to the austere satisfaction of duty accomplished and of a quiet conscience lulled to rest by a luxurious belief in a 'Better Future'. If one made allowance for the special prohibitions imposed by their religion, our conceptions of good and evil were very similar to those of the Lutherans and the Pietists. There were simply 'the things one should do' and 'the things one did not do'; these were determined either by the will of God or by human wisdom, according to the outlook of the person involved. But all, believers and unbelievers, carried the same burden towards the same end, their road being brightened at long intervals by a marriage feast set beneath the trees

on some fine summer's day to tunes played on a con-
certina.

I do not recall that we went in for questioning things.
To some, religion had already given the answers and to
ask questions would have seemed indiscreet, while for
the others there was no one source from which answers
could be expected.

YES, I was a happy child and, all in all, not difficult to please. A pencil and a few sheets of paper ensured the peace of those around me. When my paper was used up, I drew on the back of the oilcloth, on the back of the chairs, in fact on anything which could be drawn on without damaging it. I drew people, trains, complicated arabesques, all of which were greatly admired by my family. A drawing seemed to them to have something magic about it, for here was reality caught in a net and landed on the blank page; this catch was the equivalent of a fine fish taken from nowhere. I was never left short of pencils.

In those days the middle class was very suspicious of any talent for art (an outlook which has changed into respectful stupefaction since canvases have become a way of hoarding money and their prices have touched astronomical heights), while, on the contrary, simple people were deeply impressed by anyone who had a gift for drawing. This, indeed, set him apart and made of him a person to be humoured.

When one is short of everything, the means of expression, too, are lacking and drawing is the one that gives most satisfaction and attracts most attention.

I have often wondered from whom I inherit this gift, which seemed to be unknown in my family. Perhaps it was only the consequence of my natural laziness which caused me to bring the world into my home and thus relieve me of the need to go out to visit it.

However this may be, my habit of remaining for hours in front of a sheet of paper, on which life and movement refused to appear, gave me an early taste for being alone and this was enhanced by a considerable talent for avoiding action. Happy and easy-going, I can now see that I was exceptionally vague, so vague indeed that today I am unable to write 'I was there or this thing happened'. On the other hand, I need only a few seconds of collectedness to savour once more the sensations of all those far-off years, to taste the translucent gooseberries that grew on a bush at the entrance to the garden, to sense again the cool water of the stream touching my ankles, or to hear the sound of my grandmother humming in her kitchen; yet I do not recall a single event at which I was present. I can remember the tone of a voice but not the words that were spoken, nor can I remember anything that happened to me. Perhaps that is because my family saw to it that nothing ever did happen to me?

Well, more or less nothing, but they could not control war and peace and because of this one of my rare memories, it is also the earliest, is of the cellar in Belfort in which my mother and I were wounded by a bomb, of the then impressive weight of seven kilos. I had refused to leave my mother's skirts to take my place in the big packing-case filled with straw into which, as soon as the alert sounded, the other inhabitants of the cellar had stuffed their babies. My resistance resulted in our being thrust under the airhole. This place was considered a safe one, the idea being that any bomb fragments would fly above us without causing us any injury.

On that day several bombs fell on the town, dropped by black planes shaped like crosses which were named 'Taubes'. One of the bombs fell in front of our house and tore up seven metres of pavement. Owing to the presence of the sand-bags which had been piled up on either side of the air vent the trajectory of the bomb splinters was not at all what had been predicted and my mother and I were wounded – the only ones to be wounded in the cellar and even in the town. My mother's wound was in her right arm and mine in my left foot. I was two years old. I have retained a memory of a sort of crypt filled with shadows in which the dim light of a lamp shone on a few children huddled together in a sort of crèche.

At the hospital a doctor examined our wounds and took a very bad view of mine. He spoke of amputating my foot so as to avoid complications. In that war surgery had still a long way to go. My mother, who is the personification of firmness, threatened to throw herself out of the window with me in her arms. She was told that my tendons had been cut, that my toes could never grow, that I should have a deformed foot and likely enough I'd get gangrene as well. But such determination shone out of her blue eyes that the idea of cutting off my foot was given up. Our wounds healed and after a time we left hospital carrying our bomb fragments in a tin box itself shaped like a bomb.

In the train which was taking us back to my grand-parents an officer jingling with medals and decorations looked at our dressings, enquired about our misfortunes, cursed the barbarous Boches and, unpinning a medal, bent over me to fasten it on to my coat – or perhaps to take a better look at my mother who was very young and very blonde.

SINCE the main road by-passed us by several kilometres, we were not involved in confrontations with strangers; the military convoys missed us out, so did the caravans going to town to set up a fair, and so, for that matter, did the political cliques.

At Colombier-Châtelot not even party meetings, such as those which sometimes caused Foussemagne to unfreeze, took place.

This part of the country belonged to a marquis who ruled over it as his father and grandfather had done before him and as, no doubt, his son and grandson would. Except for the Reds, everyone voted unquestioningly for the marquis, for his personal qualities and because he was of the quality and no doubt a bit too because the humble elector was not displeased to put him under an obligation to his former churls. In any case politics smelt bad to the men of the Right; an honest man should not touch them, any more than he should drink, except in an emergency and to resist some greater evil.

The left-wingers obviously held quite the opposite view; they regarded politics as the highest activity of the human mind and the finest career, except for that of medicine.

It was thanks to politics that my parents had met. My mother, who had an enquiring mind, had heard my father speak on socialism to a working-class audience near Belfort. She had a combative spirit, a fine voice and the enthusiasm of her twenty-five years. Out of love of socialism she followed my father from meeting to meeting and eventually into the registry office. When she told me this story it didn't mean much to me for, so far as I was concerned, my parents had always been my parents and I couldn't imagine that, at some time in their lives, they might not have become my parents.

The honesty, the decency of their married life made me believe that marriage was something which couldn't be undone and, for this reason, that it had had no beginning.

My parents shared a little flat with another tenant; it looked out on to a Belfort street, which, in the far distance, ended in a piece of wasteland covered with dusty grass. My mother sold the paper of the socialist federation on the street, my father had edited the entire text. He was a former teacher who had been sacked and reduced to destitution for his revolutionary activities. But politics were everything to him.

He used to say that he had taken to politics as a duck takes to water. By the age of ten he had already made his choice: he was going to be a journalist and a member of parliament.

He did not wait to become a journalist; sitting on a public bench, he concocted every evening, for his own pleasure and that of his school-friends, a newspaper called *The Boer*. It was written on packing paper and paid homage to the republicans of the Transvaal, those heroes of a now-forgotten colonial war.

By the time he was thirteen he had become the correspondent of a provincial paper which was published in the east of France. One day its editor-in-chief conceived the good democratic idea of inviting all the team to a banquet. He was astonished when one of the political correspondents arrived in shorts. and he had not been sent to apologize for his father's absence! My father won an exhibition to the Government teachers' training college; he passed out of it while still of an age at which other boys were trying to gain admission. Because he was so young and moreover because he had unfortunately attracted attention to himself, not only by his letters to the local papers but also by the articles he wrote for Jean Jaurès's paper *L'Humanité*, and finally because he was always in the opposition camp at any political meeting, he was sent to a mountain school in the Vosges. It was a school which was more or less empty for two-thirds of the year; in the winter because of the snow and in the summer because of the work in the fields. He was teaching there when he was dismissed. First he was visited by a lawyer and a judge charged jointly with the task of advising him and of reprimanding him. (They had also to make out a case against him which was in fact against the spirit of the law.) They were briefed to prove that a certain unruliness in the local barracks, where the conscripts had become angry at being kept on in the army after their term of service had ended, was the result of my father's influence. They could not do so because there was no truth in the accusation, but, in any case, the investigation was no more than a formality.

It proved negative, but only three weeks later my father was dismissed in the most summary manner. Although the law did not say that teachers were forbidden to be socialists they were advised not to advertise their socialism. Middle-class society, which for so long had been sitting innocently astride the wisdom, patience and endurance of the poor, was far from happy when it began to feel that the caryatid had come to life.

Well, my father had been a socialist from the age of thirteen. He used to say that it was a speech by Jaurès which had opened the promised land to him, and that he had perceived it between the stucco arabesques of *La Belle Époque*. Like birds which fly up along the façade of some splendid cathedral and then disappear into it through a tall window, the bold young scholar of the École Normale plunged with delight into the long, sonorous history of French socialism, as described by the great orator.

Abandoning the practical questions which at that time were the concern only of the radical left-wing, my father's mind was projected by the force of Jaurès's eloquence into higher spheres. In the end he became a militant in whose opinion the solution to everything lay in politics which for him became the equivalent of what 'being' represented to the classical philosophers.

From now onwards his family were to see very little of him and the department soon became too narrow for the exercise of his talents. By the time he was twenty-nine he had risen to the post of Secretary to the Socialist Party and had established us on the fifth floor of a building in the fifteenth arrondissement of Paris. There was no lift; below us was a coal depot and next door ran the garden of a convent. My mother used to say proudly: 'We have no house facing ours.' From our balcony we could see the two top storeys of the Eiffel Tower, at that time used for advertising a firm of motor manufacturers in letters of fire.

I slept in the room that my father used during the day as his office. My bed faced a portrait of Karl Marx and stood beneath one of Jules Guesde holding a pen and a photograph of Jaurès. A doctrinaire Marxist, who was respected and listened to but not understood, Jules Guesde with his long hair and dishevelled beard looked like a willow in a rainstorm.

His rather sombre glance seemed to be avoiding that of Jaurès, who, with his beard thrust forward, was the epitome of an optimistic southern Frenchman, full of the happiness of living in a world that was soon going to be so beautiful, and of the joy of guiding so many people towards the fraternal city, of which history has made him aware and towards which a hurricane of prophecies was pushing the people.

Because of all this my socialism was a double-faced Janus whose contrasting aspects were the quiet of the study and the activity of creative improvisation; the silence of a library and the jolly process of recreation. Karl Marx fascinated me. He was a lion, a sphinx, a solar eruption. His great forehead emerged from a cloud of silver hair looking like an impenetrable tower of thought and his extremely alert glance followed anyone who contradicted him round the room till the objector was squashed. The line of his moustache gave the illusion that he was smiling the smile with which, when he was in his poor lodgings in London, he must have greeted such famous visitors as Leo Tolstoy and Élisée Reclus, both of whom in any case left without hearing one word of false politeness from him.

Jules Guesde and Jaurès belonged to their generation, the one by his melancholy, the other by his humanity. Karl Marx did not belong to any age. There was something indestructible about him, something that had turned to stone – it was the certainty of being right.

This solid block of dialectic watched over my childish slumbers.

SINCE my parents had no one to leave me with, from the age of five I used to go with them to Le Mur des Fédérés which was the traditional rendezvous of revolutionary processions. I saw this wall under snow and in sunshine, covered with mud and covered with flowers. It seemed to be the world's end, the end of the dyke where the human flood crashed and broke in the scarlet foam of bouquets and banners.

I had learned to sit below the platform for hours on end while speeches flew over my head like black thunderclouds chasing before them the flags and the miseries of the world. In front of me hundreds of weeping eyes were raised as the people listened to the tale of their misfortunes.

Then the speakers stopped, silence fell, and the wind swirled the red tongues of the flags and the murmur of a resurrection still to be rose from the ground: 'Up crowd of slaves . . .' This curious chant rolled like thunder, bearing great hopes but it never reached the pitch of joy. All eyes were filled with a kind of prayer which was joined to a refusal. The Internationale was sung with the pauses and rushes of a litany.

Socialism was living through its age of faith.

*

It was a religion and, like any young religion, it excluded all others. It was not an economic system; the Marxists I knew who had read Karl Marx were no more numerous than the Catholics who had read the *Summa Theologica* of St Thomas Aquinas. Marxism was a faith: mankind was good (though this was not always true of men), and now man had taken the matter of his salvation in hand. Our Jaurès and our Jules Guesde were regarded with as much reverence as Christians pay to the Fathers of the Church. Karl Marx was the Moses of the proletarians in exile; he was going to lead us out of the Egypt of conformity and submission. True, he himself had disappeared long ago into the fogs of London but the violence of his thought was still with us and would inevitably bear us to that world of reconciliation whose advent he had predicted. We were brothers, not only by reason of a faith held in common, but by the blood of unending human sacrifice made throughout millennia of injustice.

The traditional religions also held that all men were brothers but our view of fraternity was not quite like theirs. They endowed men with a common father; our fraternity, sincere and deep as it was, did not recognize any father, we were 'fraternal orphans'. No doubt that was why, instead of calling each other 'brothers', we greeted each other as 'comrades'.

*

Socialism was a new church and my father was one of its youngest and most gifted acolytes. His mother had given him the hyphenated forename of 'Louis-Oscar' but the comrades called him Ludovic. I don't know why this was, perhaps they thought that this formerly romantic

name suited his pensive appearance, his precocious bald-
ness, his eyeglass, and his myopic stare.

His talent for drawing the significance out of any piece
of political information and his capacity for making an
analysis or a motion or for writing an article had made
him an essential member of any committee. His intelli-
gence bought time and his memory served instead of
archives. Improbable as it may seem, he was able to name
the six hundred French constituencies and quote the
number of votes received by each candidate in the two
rounds of the poll. He could also provide the dates of
birth and death of any important person whose name one
might chance on in any encyclopedia. All his books, in
which references to events and speeches are numerous,
were written from memory. When he spoke in public or
addressed the Assembly he never used a note, though his
speeches were often long and their construction was
admirable. He usually began in a voice that vibrated with
unexpected emotion allied to irony but ended in a ham-
mering gallop.

In the Chamber of Deputies it was his duty to welcome,
in the name of his group, the Ministers who were about
to take office. Some of them, it is said, never recovered
from this or their baptism which was administered to the
accompaniment of sarcastic clouts.

Since he spoke so much outside he didn't speak once
he was inside our house. He left early in the morning and
returned late at night. He dined alone on hard-boiled
eggs, salad, baked potatoes and nuts which it amused him
to crack between his teeth, all the while deep in thought,
his eyes fixed on the table-cloth or on the paper which lay
folded in four by his plate. I used to cross the room on

the tips of my toes holding my breath and make my way timidly round this monument of mental concentration.

Occasionally, in the summer, he felt the need to breathe his native air. As soon as he had arrived he would go out fishing, his rod on his shoulder, a wicker basket lined with leaves in his hand, and make his way to the little river that ran near to the village between rushes and weeds. We used to choose the most shady spot even if it was not the one where there were the most fish. He would cast his line and then roll one of those cigarettes the paper of which burned more slowly than the tobacco, so that it ended up as a charred funnel at the corner of his mouth. Then he would go and lie with his back against a tree and his cap over his nose and instruct me to keep an eye on the float and to let him know if there were a bite, which didn't happen very often.

After a damp hour in the scorching meadow we made our way home with a couple of little fish jumping around in our basket. Afterwards my aunt would fry them, rejoicing in the bonus added to our menu.

At table our conversation was in the 'Belfort' style; that is to say every quarter of an hour we uttered a word carefully chosen so that it did not require any response. The presence of the head of the family with his growing fame as an orator and as a politician made us hold our tongues, while his talent for repartee encouraged us to be prudent.

We were loaded to the lips with admirable views, so well loaded indeed that we were like cannon that no one dared fire. Trappist monks are more talkative than we were and because we never said anything, all words seemed empty to us, and we felt better able to communicate with each other without using them.

My uncle occasionally allowed himself a remark such as 'How're you getting on over there?', which seemed to comprise an enquiry that was both impersonal and reasonably solicitous and also took in the past, the present and the future. It included the elder brother who had gone 'over there' – to Paris – to win his spurs. To this my father replied with a wry expression suggesting a judicious combination of moderate satisfaction laced with scepticism concerning all things political, the right mixture to ensure that his family, who never knew whether things were going well or badly, would be informed and at the same time reassured.

But when, as was the custom, the neighbours came to share our myrtle or rhubarb pie and drink coffee, then my father became another man. His need to explain and to convince made his face, which was usually expressionless, light up. His well-cut hands tapped the corner of the table or his index finger denounced the opposing argument and his huddled-up attitude no longer suggested a person wrapped in meditation but rather a man poised to leap forward. He took as much trouble to win over this humble audience as he did to gain the votes of the Legislative Assembly and we were amazed to see that a man who was normally so calm and undemonstrative should be capable of suddenly releasing so much energy and passion.

We saw him now as he really was, as he was when he was away from us, we saw the change that politics wrought in him. We understood that he was dedicated to an ideal and we had the vague apprehension that this ideal was never going to let go of him and restore him to us.

He was totally detached, he never made a move which could have been to his material advantage, even though for a long time now he had feared that, in spite of his reputation, he would once again know the days of destitution he had endured after he had been sacked from the teaching profession. I am sure that if war had not chased him out of the little lodging in which he was then living he would have remained there till his death.

He very seldom intervened in our daily life and when he did so it was usually to say that he was *not* going to do so. Once indeed he instructed my mother to take back to the toyshop the box of tin soldiers that I had been given for Christmas; it was exchanged for an improving game about electricity. As a socialist he could not countenance a society built on the balance of armed power. In our world there were not to be any soldiers.

One of the great surprises of my childhood was to learn that Soviet Russia had an army complete with ranks and uniforms and discipline. 'Was it possible', I asked, 'that over there too people took such a pessimistic view of human nature that soldiers were needed?'

'No', I was told. It was simply a question of being encircled by the powers of evil. Anyway, the Soviet army was known as the Red Army, and indeed I imagined that even the men were painted red, which of course made it quite different from any other army.

SOVIET RUSSIA attracted my father as it attracted all the socialists of his generation. One day he went off with Marcel Cachin, the editor of *L'Humanité*, to negotiate the eventual affiliation of the French Socialist Party to the Third International. They carried their provisions in a suitcase. The journey via the Baltic, Stettin and Helsinki took two weeks. But the *cordon sanitaire* set up by the bourgeois powers made it impossible to reach the homeland of socialism by any other route. In Moscow they met the principal protagonists of what my father called the 'event of the century'.

They were dazzled by its fire which was still burning. They listened to Lenin's admonitions and to the sour speeches in which he scoffed at the bourgeois character of the Second International and of the Third and commented on the ideological impotence of *L'Humanité*, in which he said he had never seen an item related to socialism, except for the subscription column.

Stunned by the fuss made by the doctrinaires, who overloaded them with aphorisms and advice, and bewildered by the complicated ballet of Slav negotiations, the two men also suffered from various unexpected changes of approach, which resulted in their finding themselves received icily one day and hugged on the next.

All the same, here was a place where for the first time a country had gone socialist and the most deprived class, through the action of its political *avant-garde*, now held power. Marxism had moved out of its dogmatic dream into the life of a great people.

For the socialist of the French school there was a lot that was surprising and even worrying in the Russian way of exploiting an idea much more systematically and much more strictly than the French would have thought of doing; also, the Russians were far less aware of individual shades of opinion, of which the Western meetings took account even in their most modest forms. And then there were the horrors of the civil war which was still going on in the form of purges. Yet all these problems vanished in face of the spectacle of the city of the future being built in front of their very eyes by workmen whose lineage stemmed from the Convention of 1893 and even from the Commune.

When the two pilgrims returned to France their hearts had been won and their heads provided them with reasons for their conversion.

At the congress which took place soon afterwards two-thirds of those present supported their appeal to choose affiliation to the Third International. This event was called the Secession of Tours. My father became the first secretary-general of the French Communist Party.

Certainly these events made little impact upon my virtuous childhood, but Comrade Charles Rappoport came less often to see us and I was sorry about this. Of all the leaders he was my favourite because of his Santa Claus beard, his laugh and his jovial personality which suggested that of a vegetarian ogre. But he belonged to another party, it was that of Léon Blum. We liked Blum too for he had the tact to treat children as though they were grown-ups and not to behave as though he himself were a child when he was with them.

Most often of all we went to Marcel Cachin's house. His wife, a tough American, used to pick me up in her arms and subject me to all sorts of affectionate demonstrations for which our way of life at Belfort had not prepared me. Her strength was frightening but at the same time it was reassuring; for me the Party consisted of her and the Wall and a dim place in the Rue Grange-Batelière, which was built, so they told me, over an underground river; I couldn't imagine how the river ran in the darkness under the streets of Paris. Did it run beneath arches? Were there oarsmen on the Batelière? The fate of this imprisoned water gave me nightmares.

WHEN they had cut my curls and taught me to read, the first book I was given was the *Roman de Renart*, quickly followed by *Petit Pierre sera socialiste*.

So far as I can remember, this was an ideological variant of *Tour de France de deux enfants*, edited so as to introduce children to the principles of Marxist thought.

Little Peter asked questions on his travels and so grew to learn the truth about social facts which included the slavery of the proletariat and the lack of justice in a society founded on the exploitation of the poor by a possessing class which owned all the means of production, that is to say the land and the tools and the machines and the money. Moreover this class obtained all the profit earned by the work of others and this profit they invested in further interest-bearing acquisitions which made the rich richer and the poor poorer and more numerous.

The consequence of all this was a state of permanent tension between the possessing class and the proletariat which was called the class war; periodically it led to revolts which the laws were framed to put down.

From time immemorial all institutions had been conceived and set up by the privileged class in order to perpetuate their privilege; even their ethics was designed to bind their consciences to uphold the established order, against all justice, for justice was despised by capitalism and had been banished to the future by religion.

But it was not long before Little Peter discovered that there was a remedy to this great evil, which was as old as history itself; the remedy was called *the socialization of the means of production and of exchange*. When this was brought about there would be a radical change in human relationships, indeed they would be purified from all that now caused them to be pernicious and iniquitous. Human relationships would no longer be based on the slave/master pattern or that of the oppressor and the oppressed; all relations would be as between man and man and based on complete equality. General dispossession would be decreed by law in favour of the collectivity. On goods produced by the workers the community would raise what was needed to give each according to his work until the day came when the community became rich enough to give to each according to his need.

Avidity, the wish to acquire and to dominate, finding no foothold, much less encouragement, in the new society, would die of atrophy. Economic and social rivalries having gone, together with the conditions which had made them inevitable, war would become pointless and would therefore disappear from the face of the earth. The members of the former possessing class would one day be transformed into human beings and the workers would recover their dignity, together with the full possession of their persons. Morality would cease to be a penal code of resignation and the religious edifices, deprived of their foundations, would collapse.

I am not claiming to have described Marxism completely in one page; it is more than likely that I have mixed it up with my early lessons and with the pages of my big red book. But anyway, Little Peter became a socialist and, since he was a nice boy and very serious, so did I.

I HAVE said it already: God did not exist; but there are various modes of not existing.

For those who happily distributed old tracts which listed the twelve proofs that God does not exist (adding an extra seven to the normal five of the Christian apologists) the imaginary being called God had simply been invented by the priests. 'God' was no more than an arbitrary term which had been chosen by the clergy to explain cause and effect, or a rather childish way of calling out 'eureka' before the book of nature had been read to its end. These characters wore big black hats. They were mildly surprised to learn that Robespierre, who seemed in his person to incarnate the very spirit of Revolution, should so often have referred to a *Supreme Being* who seemed to have some points in common with the God of the religions that had been abolished. But perhaps it was because of his need for the absolute that Robespierre had chosen to terminate his work in the region of heaven. The place had remained dangerously uninhabited and so he had established an anonymous Being there, not so far removed from *Le Grand Être* of pagan times. The Supreme Being had no attributes, held no responsibilities, but was a sort of premise of the natural order. That was how they explained Robespierre's deism.

To others the existence of God was not only inconceivable but also inadmissible, for it would have placed at the origin of everything, between creator and creations, an inequality so intrinsic that it would have made confrontation unnecessary and dialogue impossible.

The act of creation imposes a form on all creation and this form conditions the laws which will govern its state. But the people I am talking about found it impossible to accept any law; laws were there to be opposed. By attributing everything to chance and energy they removed the need for laws. For them, too, what chance had given birth to could be unmade without contravening the decrees of any almighty Power.

For many of them religion was a primitive way of explaining experiences and it would disappear with the progress of knowledge. Because they did not know the causes of natural phenomena, the early peoples had attributed them to supernatural powers which they thought it expedient to conciliate. God, then, was only the projection of all they could not understand. The more they knew, the less they would believe, so it was clear enough that the sphere of religion would diminish in proportion to the expansion of the sphere of science. Religion would cease to exist on the day, believed to be not far off, when everything would be explained.

Those who held this view would not agree that after anything has been explained there is a still greater need for an explanation. To this argument against religion could be added (if the need arose, but it seldom did) the suffering of the innocent and the imperfection of the Church.

Anti-clericalism no longer played the important part which it had played at the beginning of the twentieth century. The separation of Church and State had very effectively separated the antagonists who had now chosen different fields in which to confront each other.

Also, small groups of Christians, having broken with the tradition which had kept them on the Right in politics, now called themselves democrats – and they even made a real effort to be good democrats. We thought they were well-meaning without taking them seriously.

During the second congress in Moscow a Dutch delegate had been greeted with loud laughter when he put forward, for which post I have forgotten, the name of a candidate who was described as a Christian communist. After having been entertained by this contradiction in terms, the congress proceeded to other business and my father, though he was no sectarian, wrote in his notebook that the Dutch joke was a bit stupid.

We could not imagine that people who were subject to a hierarchy which gave utterance to binding dogmas, who were obliged to confess (self-criticism was not yet on our statute-book), whose intimate thoughts were liable to be investigated by a priest, could ever be democratic in the sense in which we understood democracy; that they could be communists was even more unthinkable.

All the same religion no longer aroused our passions and we did very little '*curé*-eating', even during big feasts.

WE rejected everything connected with Catholicism, with the notable exception of the human person of Jesus Christ. Towards him the older members of the Party retained a rather chary feeling that he stood for the birth of ethics and had a poetic destiny.

We didn't belong to him but he could very well have belonged to us because of his love of the poor, his censure of those in power and above all because he had been a victim of the priests, or at least of the Establishment, in fact, the victim of power and its machinery of repression.

My father was not unwilling to recite, for the benefit of his friends, a poem by Jehan Rictus called 'If he came back'. Its theme, told in simple language, was that of Christ coming back to our world. The point made was that if he came back everything would happen over again in just the same way except that the middle class, having learned its lesson, would see to it that Christ did not become a martyr; they would deal with him equally efficiently by describing him as a dreamer and gently smothering him.

One thing was certain: he would never enter the homes of those who pretended to belong to him. He would never be seen inside a church, but more likely in the police station among the dregs of society.

This dirge expressed a certain protective tenderness

towards Christ and a pity that was near to compassion:

The wound of the spear is still in your side.

This opening made by the spear in the side of the crucified Christ was a further indictment of bourgeois society, and my father read this particular passage with exceptional feeling.

The general opinion was that if its mythical superstructure were removed, the Gospel could pass as a reasonably good introduction to socialism. We were even willing to admit this to any Christians who pressed the point. But, having made this concession, we were more than surprised that they did not immediately become socialists. As for our becoming Christians, such an idea never entered our minds. Anything that had preceded socialism had merely heralded its birth. Our faith sufficed us. Since it was bound to the very movement of history it appeared to be irrefutable. (And, indeed, might not the only way of refuting Marxism be to practise it?)

The believer imagines, usually falsely, that the unbeliever concerned with the problems of life and death must suffer from his inability to receive any replies to the many questions which harass him, in spite of the prohibition of such doubts by the scientific outlook. But for the unbeliever life is a matter for the scientists; one day they will be able to create it and so deliver man from death.

Also, it must be understood that collectivism is not simply a theory of economics, it is also a true form or mysticism which affords its adherents a kind of impersonal immortality. If someone were to live totally for the community what, at the end of his life, would he have to lose? The jaws of death would snap on nothingness. Having

75

given up everything to the community, he would in some way survive in the community, to which for years he had, in any case, delegated his judgment and his will.

The collectivist mystic can lose himself in the collectivity as the Christian mystic can lose himself in God. The difference is that the collectivist does not find himself again.

THIS is not a confession. I could not write that sort of book, for the sunburst of July, which I shall describe later, has blotted out of my mind almost all that happened before. The impressions of childhood stick, indeed they are so deep that they resist even old age, but the impressions left by my adolescent years are no more than vague spots of colour such as dance before one's eyes when one has been looking into the sun.

What kind of boy was I between the ages of ten and twenty? No doubt much the same as other boys of that age, yet, apart from the peculiarities of my background, I was different in certain ways and these were not to my credit.

Because my father had been a brilliant scholar it was assumed that I would resemble him in this. What a mistake, but all the more excusable because at the start I did very well.

At my primary school all went satisfactorily. We came from humble backgrounds, anyhow we looked as though we did for we all wore identical black pinafores and our masters' views on life were the same as those of our parents. They taught us gravely as was then the custom among the dispensers of learning; knowledge was a fairly new boon and still a surprise to the poorer classes, for whom education was the only asset they possessed.

For us, history was forging its way between good and evil, under a heaven almost entirely occupied by Victor Hugo. It was helped forward by virtue, held back by ignorance, but was going towards those happy ends which had been predicted by the best and most prescient of men. Freedom led to the ideals of universal goodness and brotherhood and these were not just ideals held by our masters, and consequently by ourselves, but they were also the ideals of the Republic and of the climate of those times. To be free, all one need do was to learn – so we learned and we were taught with patience and in great detail by exemplary teachers who were aware that their books contained the secret of all success.

I had good marks and the little black velvet bag which hung from my neck by a cord and looked rather like a scapular was always filled with small squares of yellow, blue and red, which represented these awards. If one gained a given number of those dockets one was awarded the Cross of Honour. I often wore it, for in spite of my absent-mindedness I had a facility for work.

One day I was given a dictation from Mérimée. It was probably from this that my subsequent disasters stemmed. I made only one mistake, I had always thought that the word *alvéole* (cellular) was feminine since femininity seemed suited to its form and purpose.

This success confirmed my teachers' view that I was outstandingly gifted. My father already saw me attending a teachers' training college, sent to an important post, becoming a professor of history; I was going to be all he could have been had not his poverty obliged him to take a short-cut. My headmaster and my other masters went into conference, they met one evening at the home of their one-time colleague, my father. They decided to send me to a secondary school. I entered the first form of the upper school at the age of nine and a half.

This was much too early; the way of teaching, the type of lesson, were new to me, but what was really fatal was the change in milieu. In my first school all my school-fellows were like myself, my cousins and my friends; we lived the same kind of life and when lessons were over we played in the dreary Paris streets which were as alike as two pins to the dreary streets of Belfort.

The secondary school stood on the edge of a rich neighbourhood, where the houses had lifts. My school-fellows wore ties and had already learned from their parents, if not the ways of the world, at least how to make their way into spheres which, though they had not yet entered them, they knew by instinct they would inherit.

The teaching I received was not intended to make me free but to instruct me in the art of dominating. Of course I could not then have defined what I felt but I realize now that this is certainly what I did feel

The primary school was an institution which belonged to the public, its masters were the heirs of the wise men of the past, they were the equals of the Encyclopedists and we owed them our complete attention and our gratitude. The secondary school was a mansion (and it was not my family mansion) in which a professor had succeeded the nanny as a dispenser of wisdom and had acquired very little prestige in doing so.

The self-confidence of my school-fellows, who worked with unconcern but played with enthusiasm, the sarcasm of the professors who called us 'Sir' in a ridiculously

ceremonial manner and emphasized their politeness towards us in proportion to our ignorance, the fact that I
was taught different subjects in different class-rooms by
different masters, all this upset me and filled me with
anxiety.

When I saw the great walls of the school and its
enormous barred windows, I became still more appre-
hensive and it was with genuine childish despair that I
used to enter this large cage in which I knew there were
no friends to make me welcome.

When I was not being frightened at the thought of the
questions they might ask me I was frightened that they
might not question me. If I had to stand up to give an
answer, I felt dizzy, my head became emptied of the
little knowledge it might once have harboured, I lost my
voice and stood silent in an atmosphere of general com-
miseration.

I can't remember ever having played with any of the
boys. They ran around, occasionally shoving me to some
other place as though I were an unwanted piece of
furniture. Sometimes I tore madly about the yard so as
to look as though I were taking part in the fun, indeed I
put so much energy into this act that I twice fell and cut
my forehead.

In the end I gave up both games and lessons. I developed a certain talent for disappearing and wandering
about the streets and the parks in the company of Voltaire and Jean Jacques Rousseau. Adventures in philosophy
were to my taste and until I was thirty I had never read
any novels excepting Voltaire's and those could more
properly be called pamphlets. I was dazzled by the acute
perceptions and irrepressible spirit of the author of *Candide*.

I saw him as some magnificent swashbuckler advancing across his age, sword in hand, pursuing a great helter-skelter of tyrants, unworthy judges and furious, frightened clerics. I am sure that I read his *Dictionary of Philosophy* ten times over, I was enchanted by his definitions and found what I now regard as their facetious banter the height of elegance.

For Rousseau I had an even greater affection. He was less inclined to hold one at arm's length and, under the tinsel of his author's vanity, one could guess at the suffering of a genius who could not come to terms with life and had no other way of coping with the situation in which he found himself than to change a world in which he did not feel at home. Rousseau may have believed himself to be better than he would in fact have enjoyed being but, unlike Voltaire, he was very ill at ease in 'society' and the snubs that came his way endeared him to me. I could imagine him being even more unhappy than I was at the school which I was now attending so infrequently.

Thanks to an excessive but brief annual sweat I succeeded for some time in rising from one form to the next. Then came the day when there was more ground to make up than I could manage to cover.

My mother became alarmed. The Vice-Principal, a man who looked like an Assyrian and had a vast chest, raised his hands to heaven and in a resounding voice explained to my parents that whether or not I happened to be present in class made no difference for I was always intellectually absent and that for this reason it was useless to correct me because I was not able to take in what was said to me.

While he was speaking, I realized that I had no recollection of any reprimand being addressed to me or of any sign of interest being shown in me, so surely this proved that what the Vice-Principal was saying must be the truth.

My father became very thoughtful and one day summoned me to the foot of his bed (he spent a lot of time on his bed reading, writing, and composing his speeches, amid a whirl of newspapers); he spoke to me with the voice of reason, he might as well have addressed his words to someone stone-deaf.

It was only much later that I realized what a disappointment I had been to him, how sad I had made him. Children know a lot but they can't know what it is like to have a child.

My mother refused to admit that I had any intellectual limitations. If I seemed to have developed some deficiencies, these could only, in her opinion, be due to the fact that I was growing fast, to the stupidity of my teachers or to the climate of Paris, to any cause, in fact, except some lack on my part, for what, she asked, could possibly be the matter with someone who loved painting and music as much as she did herself. Maternal love accepted all my excuses and even supplied me with others which had not occurred to me.

I lived for drawing and, to some extent, by drawing. Give me paper, a pen and Indian ink and I was happy. Under the lasting influence of the *Iliad* (which neither Voltaire nor Jean Jacques Rousseau had displaced in my affections), I drew nothing but Greek temples, copied from a book on Hellenic architecture.

The white page represented light and my thousands of

little black etchings limited the space and obliged the form to appear. Hoping to compel it to become visible earlier, inexperienced as I was, I sometimes doubled the number of my lines till they grew into palisades behind which the imprisoned form remained forever hidden. My aim was to make objects speak up and declare their identity, but a few strokes too many often ruined my efforts and the white column which I had intended to call forth vanished under a barrage of scribbles. I tore up the sheet of paper, I tried again, ten times, a hundred times.

Noting my perseverance, my mother, who never understood my talents, remembered that Courbet too was from Franche-Comté and that our village was proud of having given birth to an excellent painter called Hoggar. I was evidently their heir and obviously our province was destined to supply France with artists.

One of our former neighbours – he now lived in Paris and had in his time written some agreeable love-songs – suggested that I might try to get in to the École des Arts Décoratifs. He was sure that I would be accepted and he was right. My name appeared towards the top of the list while I was still a few months under the minimum age for entrants.

My father, having decided to be content with the little I was capable of doing, showed in his own discreet way that he was pleased. He took me to the distant island of Martinique which he had represented in the Assembly for the previous two years.

During the twelve or thirteen days we were at sea we only spoke to each other about five or six times and then our remarks were so loaded with the cargo of things we had never said that they went straight to the bottom of the silence through which we usually cruised.

At Fort-de-France hundreds of boats, all of them be-flagged, were awaiting our arrival under a blazing sky. From the time we landed our feet never touched the ground till night fell, for we were chaired from husting to husting by an enthusiastic, laughing crowd and, please believe me, in spite of their great poverty, these people had great natural dignity.

During the following days, while my father carried out his hard task, getting wages raised and fighting ad-ministrative red-tape, an erudite professor of geography, who fortunately had a good sense of humour, took me round the island. He instructed me in its history, showed me the 'bread tree' and the 'butter tree' and warned me against the manchineel, which makes people go blind. I saw one very pretty sight: a pineapple grove at dusk; and also a terrifying sight: Mount Pelée throwing up large incandescent rocks into the night sky.

In the evening, sitting under the flower-decked verandahs amid the buzzing of cockchafers, which flew from one lamp to another, we were waited on by very pretty girls. I admired their svelte figures, their profiles lit up by a ray of light, and could hardly have imagined a happier fate than to spend the rest of my life at their feet.

Our visit, which was delightful but also harassing, lasted a month. By that time I quite understood why my father spoke so little at home, obviously he had no strength left. I had always respected his silence and after this trip I began to respect his personality. On the ship which was taking us back to France we again became mutes, but those few weeks spent together had helped us to understand each other.

We had never had need of words to communicate, a gesture or a glance had sufficed; now, given the further knowledge we had of each other, we were able to cut down even on these.

WHEN I returned to Paris I went to the École des Arts Décoratifs but I was no more assiduous at my classes there than I had been at school. For so many years I had rejected all discipline that by now I was unable to keep to a time-table. I was also incapable of following any plan of study; for instance, I was not prepared to draw models selected so as to help those of us who had little talent to acquire at least some technique.

I was not keen on becoming a designer; perhaps my taste was neither sure enough nor bad enough? I would have liked to have become an architect (even though the term 'architect' was a term of abuse among the art students), always provided that I would be allowed to build Greek temples.

It was even easier to play truant from the Arts Décoratifs than it had been to absent oneself from the *lycée*; I therefore spent most of my time in the parks and the swimming-pools, or at exhibitions, where I made straight for the architectural section.

In the Louvre my preference was for pictures with architectural backgrounds, if possible in the Attic style.

I also shyly sought out the company of girls, to whom, if the opportunity occurred, I offered my platonic devotions. However, on my fifteenth birthday, being in funds, I thought it appropriate that I should spend the evening with a lady of the town and I took the metro to Montparnasse to pursue this purpose.

When I arrived at my destination I saw, sitting at the end of the underground passage, an emaciated beggar who looked as though he had been painted in pitch against a white tiled background. (The effect was rather like that of the figures of the Matisse chapel at Vence.) As I passed in front of him I realized that I wasn't going any further in my search for adventure – not that night anyway.

Was I moved by pity, by the cruelty of the contrast between this man forced to beg and the furtive roisterer I was preparing to become, was it an impulse to do something unexpected, or the relief at not having to go forward with an experience for which I hadn't the guts? I don't know what my motive may have been, but the packet of notes in my pocket fell into the beggar's cap and I went back to have my return ticket punched.

(Unfortunately when advancing along the wrong road I have not always met a beggar to divert me!)

*

My good actions were very rare, partly because I was unable to identify myself with any circle or group, and in consequence I was rapidly going wild. My mother often had to suffer from my bad temper; the gentle, silent child on whom people who liked a quiet life used to compliment her, had vanished. His place had been taken by an aggressive half-wit who was concerned with his muscular development, who spent his mornings in a warm swimming-bath, who accepted no advice or admonitions and who was very cross with his young sister. Moreover, this idiot felt quite capable of teaching himself, and to this end he accumulated a number of books on philosophy, of which, in the event, he has not remembered one line.

My mother who, like many others, felt more responsible for my failures than for my successes tried to convince my father that my disorderly existence was due to my having joined the world of artists. He doubted this. He said he did not think I would ever be any good at anything.

All the same, he tried to make me do something. By now, having spent several years trying unsuccessfully to acquire the spirit of mortification imposed on communist leaders by the hierarchy, he had returned to the socialist fold. Now he proposed that I should found a group of young socialists in the little mining town in eastern France of which he had become the deputy and also the mayor.

I drew up statutes, I acquired enrolment cards. I made a speech on the theme 'We are entering the field while our elders are still in possession of it'. Thirty boys listened to me, afterwards thirty boys joined the Party. The group had got off to a flying start. Thereafter I allowed it to continue on its way without me. Never again was I seen at its head or at its tail.

My prospects, from being depressing, had become hopeless.

I AM sorry to have to inflict such a long account of my uncertain and lazy beginnings on my readers, but since I have to describe the way in which I received an arbitrary grace, I need also to show that it might just as well have come to someone more deserving. Perhaps this will also satisfy those who have complained to me that they have never experienced the encounter that I was destined to have. Very likely they were considered quite capable of making the discovery for themselves, whereas my weakness required a revelation.

*

In everyone's opinion my father's career was bound to lead him to the highest political posts. As it turned out, he became a Minister in a government which lasted for twenty-four hours. They were very impressive those twenty-four hours, both to him and to us. We went to visit him in his glory; he was installed in a charming house on the Left Bank and looked sufficiently surprised to find himself in an eighteenth-century mansion instead of in the eighteenth arrondissement. He was quite unimpressed by the tapestries or the gilt of the state furnishings; indeed, he had accepted the post of Minister only out of a sort of humility, as though having already made a name for himself, without knowing it, he now felt the need of an address.

I am quite sure that the happiest moments of his political life were those spent in little cafés of his constituency where, in the evenings before supper, he would play cards, between the counter and the glass door, with miners who had just come out of the depths and whose eyes were only gradually readjusting themselves to light and space.

Here, at last, he could be himself – I know it and they knew it.

*

Busy as he was, he remained on the alert for any sign of talent that I might improbably display.

A celebrated left-wing cartoonist having drawn my attention to the fact that a newspaper is first and foremost a picture in black and white and that any drawing intended to be reproduced in it should be related to the typography in which it will be framed, I made an effort to put this advice into practice and drew some caricatures of politicians.

My father took them to the party paper which added me to its staff, all the more readily because it needed his support. One of my victims even went so far as to ask me to send him my original drawing and wrote me a personal letter of thanks. As he was a former *Président du Conseil*, this brought me some prestige. Since I could draw it was supposed that I could also write and indeed a short story I had written at the age of fifteen was accepted by a well-known periodical and appeared in a prominent position in it.

Our friends forgot that I owed these honours to my

father's recommendations and began to recall that there had been some great writers as lacking in qualifications as I was. (I remained without qualifications for many years, in fact until the day on which I became a naval officer.) True, the number of such authors was not very large, but it was assumed that with a little good-will my name could surely be added to theirs. Our friends were prepared to wait for a while for this to happen.

By now I had become an expert in the art of disappointing. If someone showed interest in my Greek temples, I was busy drawing caricatures; if these were accepted, then the paper should instead publish my stories; but if they thought they had got hold of a fiction-writer they were mistaken for by that time I was canoeing on every lake around Paris. In the end, my father put a stop to all this by insisting that I should earn my living.

Since I had no idea how to begin, he placed me on the staff of an evening paper which was edited by a friend of one of our cousins. I was seventeen at the time. Among my colleagues were several old hands and one or two sons of notabilities; all were older than I. I was allocated to 'crime' and told to get the know-how by helping more experienced reporters.

The men with whom I went to the police station, to the scene of the crime or to the morgue, kindly helped me to acquire that mixture of scepticism and *naïveté* which turns the reporter into a fellow who has seen all there is to see but who is nevertheless daily astonished by events that do not surprise anyone else. Some of my companions, foreseeing that life held little for them, made the most of the freedom which their youth allowed them; they showed me evil paths along which I gratefully followed them.

I was the last arrival, the infant of the editorial department. Everyone was kind to me and occasionally I was allowed to write an article on the falling autumn leaves or on a cat show. Very soon I was relieved, as far as was possible, of any connection with crime. My investigations had been most unrewarding; by a happy chance either the victim of the murder proved to be alive and kicking, or the suicide had bungled his job. I enjoyed being a journalist, except when I was subjected to the anger of the concierges, who were still suspicious of newspapers and more especially of the evening press with its enormous banner headlines which gave the impression that every night there had been some tremendous happening.

I was getting to know the world in the company of disillusioned experts who were especially well up in the abnormalities of both crime and unbridled success. I was living the life of an adult long before I had become one. I was like those young people who are never so childish as when they no longer wish to be children and for whom the age of legal majority is the frontier beyond which are the delights of being able to do absolutely anything one chooses.

I was just like them but, by the grace of God, I had no great ambitions. Those I had were connected with the female company I kept. These ladies were obviously touched by the role of tough guy which I tried to assume in order to give myself confidence and which they realized was quite out of character.

The good example given me by my family which,

although I did not realize it, had endowed me with certain built-in moral standards saved me from the worst excesses. All the same, I was well on the way to becoming a fine specimen of an a-social socialist when an unobtrusive quirk of fate caused me to fall into the divine ambush which I shall now describe.

THE first encounter was on the banks of the Seine, under the iron bridge that crosses the river at the level of the Gare d'Austerlitz. Here, cocooned in the noise of the metro and the lapping of the lighters, stands the Institute of Forensic Medicine. I was leaning over the parapet watching the water flowing sadly by when a colleague whom I did not know came and joined me.

He was about twenty-five or twenty-six with cropped hair and a mischievous expression. The smoke arising from the cigarette which was standing up more or less vertically between his lips made him screw up his eyes and multiplied the ironical lines of his face, all of which seemed to curl round like so many question marks. His whole personality suggested laughter restrained with difficulty. Once we had got through our conventional patter, he went on to what I will not describe as the purpose of his call, but to ask the most searching questions about my past, my present and my future – the type of question I was least well prepared to answer. Finally, he enquired: What ideals had I? This was something I had never asked myself.

I had ideas which I had inherited from my father and these had been jollied up with a slight dose of Voltairian scepticism; but ideals?

What was an ideal? I wasn't at all sure I knew what the term meant. Taken aback, I looked at the boats as they

94

passed below us, which brought to mind my favourite sport, and I replied: 'Rowing.'

The effect of my reply was startling: but for the balustrade, my interrogator would have fallen into the Seine. He laughed till the tears ran down his cheeks, till I was afraid he would suffocate. This response made me aware of the absurdity of my profession of faith.

I saw myself starting from nowhere in particular and rowing with fervent idealism for the purpose of going nowhere. I also began to laugh, but not quite so loudly.

Such joyful manifestations are not a usual occurrence in the neighbourhood of the morgue. Its door opened and the doctor appeared on the threshold, but not to complain, as I had feared, only to inform us of his findings. We took our notes and then separated. As I watched the young man go off I could see by the way his back shook that he was still laughing.

We did not meet again for a year; then by chance we found ourselves working on the same paper.

As Napoleon said, 'Chance is never purposeless'.

*

The advantage of being the son of 'a somebody' is that one can always get a job without any trouble; the disadvantage is that one can lose it as easily as one acquired it for the things that determine one's fate happen at several removes from oneself. The morning came on which I was sacked from my paper without being given any explanation. The next day my father placed me on the staff of a rival paper. It belonged to a powerful arms merchant who had left-wing sympathies. He interviewed me in his austere office near the Bourse and, having given me paternal advice, sent me along to the editorial department where he was never seen. Here, among the salaried idlers, I saw the man I had met at the morgue and to whom I had given so much entertainment.

His surname was Willemin and he shared my Christian name. We seemed to have a natural affinity; why I cannot imagine for we could hardly have been more unalike.

I was listless, vaguely bitter (the kind of bitterness that at twenty one feels is becoming to one), unsociable and a dreamer lacking dreams, whom everyone seemed to enjoy plaguing when they had nothing else to do.

Willemin had a comic sense of life which turned it into a fantastic poem in which the exigencies of rhyme predominate over those of logic. He was the third son of a teacher who came from Lorraine and was a widow. There were three boys and one girl in the family; all seemed to be academic geniuses.

The eldest was first in every subject and daily his laurel wreath sprouted new leaves. He was expected to make a name for himself in some branch of erudite research, perhaps open up new fields in mathematics or philosophy. Anyhow, there was little doubt that he would enter the Académie of his choice at the age at which the generals of the Revolution had made their entry. Alas, he decided to become a vet and devoted his spare time to folk-dancing. This was a bit of a disappointment.

The second son, a doctor, one day told his horrified students that he was suffering from a tumour of the brain. As his disease developed and required a frightening operation, which was conducted partly under his instructions, he continued to give first-hand lectures on his condition which were without precedent. Eventually he died. Obviously he was a hero.

The girl, after an impressive career at school, married a mining engineer and went off with him to Alès.

My friend, the youngest, had had a rather less straightforward youth. He had given up medicine for music and then, after winning a prize as a flautist, had abandoned music for journalism.

His mother became worried and followed him to Paris. She arrived well stocked with love and wisdom and bringing with her also a certain country innocence, which caused her to thank the voice that gives the time over the telephone. Indeed, she could never get over his amiability and hated hanging up on someone who was so exaggeratedly kind as to tell her not only the hour and the minute but also the very seconds.

She was quite certain that her rather ugly duckling would, like the others, turn into a swan, and if he did not yet look quite like one this must be because she had failed him in some way. In fact his period of indecision was coming to an end. Surrounded by boys who had stopped studying, he made up his mind to go back to his books, so, while we lolled in the arms merchant's chairs waiting for a volcano to erupt somewhere, he sat in his shirt-sleeves, in a corner of the office, surrounded by high piles of medical text-books.

The two of us became something like Siamese twins and during these happy years I seemed to have acquired an elder brother who worried about my work and my health.

In the evenings, either he cooked our meal in his room, which was on the Quai Bourbon and, even if it didn't have a view on to the Seine, looked straight down on to Léon Blum's Library, or we dined under the arches of one of the bridges of the Île Saint-Louis on fried fish, indelibly stamped with the print of the newspaper in which it had been wrapped.

Willemin had been brought up a Catholic but had lost his faith at the age of fifteen. He had found it again in characteristically improbable circumstances: he had gone to a lecture by a Christian philosopher, Stanislas Fumet, and heard him praising a nineteenth-century writer called Ernest Hello. He had never heard the man's name in school, or outside it, so he said to himself: 'Since I have never heard of this celebrity, I must be very ignorant, in fact, I must be a complete ignoramus.' At which point he went off to a church and made an act of humility and felt all the better for it. He told me, without in any way convincing me, that his refound faith had brought him joy and freedom of the mind.

Since humility had done him such a good turn he tried to foster it in those he met by the simple method of drawing their attention to what donkeys they were as they trotted through the world on the frontier of infinity while remaining totally blind to it. How much they would gain, he suggested, if they followed his advice and practised the virtue of humility.

He used a lot of imagination and a lot of zest in his campaign and he never showed any pride or complacency, for he himself was completely humble, both by grace and by nature. Indeed he had the sort of humility which like charity (so the theologians say) 'spreads' itself.

Reactions were varied; many donkeys, true to their reputations, proved to be stubborn. No doubt of all the virtues which they might happen to lack, humility was the one which caused them the least inconvenience.

It goes without saying that in his eyes I was a donkey and moreover one of a particularly unhappy species: a godless, republican donkey, a Red, braying out all the propaganda with which I had been stuffed. He thought little of my views and I had no respect for his: I suspected he himself comprised the whole 'anarcho-royalist' group to which he pretended he belonged. This very improbable ideological mixture had the considerable merit of cancelling itself out so that there was no room left for argument.

In the evenings under the bridges we held long conversations which got us nowhere. Around us people talked of war, of the war which had never really ended and of the new war that would soon break out.

Daily events provided the usual carnival of crimes and absurdities, from which each of us drew his own conclusion, by attributing the frightening march-past to the activities of the left-wing or to those of the Right, according to his individual prejudice. Having registered our disagreement, we entrenched ourselves in our opposing camps but remained as inseparable as heretofore.

I doubt whether the topical events of political life occupied more place in our minds than the theme of a Breughel picture occupies on a canvas, where as a rule it has been relegated to one corner out of which it peers from between the mountains, the skies and the ocean. All the same, we never stopped talking about the Left, the Right, the Monarchy, the Republic, not that these conversations made either of us budge one inch in our views. But I think it must have been in the hope of striking a final blow at my stubborn socialism that Willemin lent me a book by Nikolai Berdyaev called *Un Nouveau Moyen Age*.

The volume, which completely failed to achieve this end, was nevertheless the cause of the misunderstanding which, in its turn, was the cause of my conversion.

I<small>T</small> is now that the central event of my life occurs. (Should I not rather say that my life begins, since, thanks to the grace of baptism, I was to know a new birth?)

It was an event which caused such an extraordinary revolution in my way of being, seeing and feeling, which altered my character so radically and made me talk in such improbable terms, that my family became alarmed.

The day before, I had been a rebellious and casual young man but there was nothing statistically unusual about me; I was quite within the norm. I gyrated in a circle of accepted opinion and as regards my sexual education, if it was disorderly, this, it was agreed, was to be expected at my age; in fact, anything could be expected of me except that I should cause astonishment. Next morning, I was a gentle youth, myself more than surprised, gravely happy and unable to prevent my happiness from spilling over on to my friends who were disconcerted at the sight of a familiar thistle suddenly sprouting roses.

It was supposed that I had been bewitched and judged expedient that I should be examined by a doctor. The one chosen was a friend, a good atheist and a good socialist. He had the sense not to suggest that I should be examined at his surgery; instead, he came to our house on a friendly visit. His questions were indirect, he did not press any point or express any curiosity; if something interested him he let a lot of conversation flow before coming back to it. We had some relaxed talks, at the end of which he gave my father his diagnosis. My condition seemed to be due to 'grace' (to the effect of 'grace'). There was nothing to worry about.

He referred to 'grace' as though it were a strange illness which could be recognized by certain well-known symptoms. The cause of the illness was as yet unknown but research into the matter was making some progress. Was it a serious illness? No, faith did not demolish reason.

Was there any known cure? No. The disease followed its course; as a rule the patient recovered. Such an attack of mysticism, occurring at my age, might be expected to last for about two years. When it had passed no scars would remain. All that was needed was patience.

My mother was reconciled. The change that had taken place in me had restored her hopes for my future, and if she had religion to thank for this she was quite enough of a realist to be grateful to it. At the start, and before he had called in the doctor, my father had been less amenable. I had asked the people who knew what had happened to keep my secret, to explain the Church to me and to have me baptized. I understood very well how displeasing it would be to a militant socialist of my father's standing to be opposed in his own home by his own son. I hoped that I had taken sufficient precautions to ensure that the details of my conversion would not feature as a piece of political gossip.

Unfortunately, someone leaked the story and it was while reading an extreme right-wing daily paper that my father learned all that was unimportant about my conversion, that is to say, everything except the true circumstances.

The paper, which showed no interest in the state of my soul, asserted that I didn't seem to value my socialist background and preferred the company of St Francis of Assisi to that of my father's friends. The point was not a very subtle one but it hit its mark. My father became convinced that the Right, aided and abetted by some artful priest, had taken advantage of the weakness of my character and of my lack of judgment to strike at him through me. He refused to see me – had he only refused to speak to me there would have been no noticeable change in our Belfortian relationship.

For some days my mother brought my meals to my room but after a time the sanctions weakened and then everything returned to normal. It was at this moment that the doctor was called in.

We arrived at a *modus vivendi*. I was allowed to indulge my religious peculiarities provided I was discreet about them and in return my family promised that they would be discreet about me. I was begged not to try to convert my young sister (nevertheless she became a Catholic, as, many years later, did my mother). I kept to my undertaking and lived with my convictions and my happiness in a sort of inner catacomb. How dearly I would have liked to share them, to spread them around me.

Whenever we were housed in the official residence of a cabinet-minister, which was now frequently the case, I used to go out, so early in the morning that the concierge was not yet at his post, to meet Willemin at the corner of the street, where he was waiting for me in his dilapidated car. Together we would go to the dawn mass at Notre-

Dame or some other church. There we usually found only one or two grey-headed women, chair-makers, wearing black straw hats. I used to look at them glued to their prie-dieu as though it were Jacob's ladder in miniature and reflect that it might be to the enduring fidelity throughout the ages of such old people that I owed the fact of finding the faith intact. I felt immensely grateful towards them, towards all those who had preserved the faith (and I might easily have added, preserved it for me), for the idea that religion might have disappeared from the earth before my arrival gave me a retrospective shiver.

Straw hats, straw-seated chairs, the grain of the Gospel, the wheat of the host – we seemed to be gathered together in a barn, where, to the sound of the new day, the priest at the altar accomplished his peaceful miracle.

After mass we went to our duties at the office. We felt like two Christopher Columbuses returning to a world that showed no interest in our discoveries. Some of our colleagues took to their heels when they saw us, others told us they had known all about religion long before we had. We doubted this, for they had so little to say about it and what they did say was so unconvincing. The great arms king sent for me, and discoursed in a kindly but alarming way about the dangers involved in mysticism should it go beyond certain limits which could easily be overstepped. Above all, let me not think of becoming a monk; the commitment would be irreversible, my parents would be driven to despair and in the end so, certainly, would I. He was thinking only of my good. Had I taken in what he was saying? Certainly I had, but his voice seemed to come from very far away, from a submerged world. He would have been surprised to know that I longed to help him.

Was there anyone with whom I could share the gift I had received? At home, our socialist friends considered me weak in the head and treated me with appropriate indulgence. In the office it was obvious that after having provided a nine days' wonder Willemin and I had now become bores. We could only exchange ideas in the corridor, which we turned into a sort of cloister. To explain our intimate conversations about the secret we shared, we invented rendezvous with imaginary people, our inversion of the old ruse whereby one conceals real love-affairs by some alibi or other.

Only one of our colleagues was at all curious about our conversations. We told him amiably that, being an unbeliever and unbaptized and wishing to stay that way, he wouldn't be able to understand what we were talking about. To this he replied that he really meant it when he said that he would be delighted to have faith.

We told him that, if this was so, all he had to do was to go to the Church of Saint-Nicolas-des-Champs, to the six o'clock mass every morning for a month, and we were quite certain that by the end of the thirty days he would be a believer. (Obviously we were very young at the time and thought we knew everything.) The man followed our advice scrupulously and went daily to the six o'clock mass. When later he joined us in the office we would greet him with 'Anything new?' To this he invariably answered in a depressed voice, 'No change.' Two weeks, three weeks passed; we became anxious. When the month had ended and he told us that he still felt no cause whatsoever to believe we were appalled.

We were greatly astonished when, on the following day, he informed us that nevertheless he had again been to mass. Just once more. No, he had no faith but he couldn't do without mass. In the event this habit continued, to that finally he became a Christian, as the result apparently of two improbable causes, envy and obstinacy.

His stubbornness brought him faith – in his own time, not ours.

We did not usually behave in such a fanciful manner, but we soon recognized that in spite of all our efforts very few people were interested in what we had to say. So far as I was concerned, I realized that no one was going to believe me and that no one was going to listen to me until I had given some proof of good sense and of my ability to live as others do, and that this entailed passing examinations and earning my living by holding a permanent job, and not by floating around. If I hoped one day to be heard, if not followed, this was what I had to do.

In other words, before proving the existence of God to others I needed to prove myself.

I should not, I thought, talk about what follows until I was regarded as a reasonable person. By then the danger would be that I should become all too reasonable; indeed, after my conversion I spent so much time proving that I was well-balanced that I nearly failed to keep my balance.

I HOPE that by now I have established the fact that nothing in my life had predisposed me towards religion, except perhaps the fact that I had none.

If my parents, from whom I had always received affection and a good example, had had faith, they would certainly have brought me up as a believer. Since they had no faith (although my mother's Protestantism had not been entirely snuffed out by socialism), it was natural that they should have brought me up to hold their views and that until I was twenty I should have shared them.

I have left out nothing concerning my youth, except that I have not dilated on the subject of adolescent problems, which good taste (now in disrepute) would formerly have prevented me from even mentioning; in any case, I have no contribution to knowledge to make in that field.

*

I am sorry to have talked so much about myself, but it wasn't possible to escape this pitfall. A very talented man, and a great one, to whom I told my story, exclaimed in astonishment when I came to the end: 'I am very fond of you, but, all the same, *why you?*' There is no answer to this question. I was a very ordinary boy with a few more weaknesses than most, but there was nothing special about me except a propensity for mental and moral absentmindedness, and when possible I was physically absent as well.

As the Scriptures say, grace has no personal preferences; in touching me it was touching just anybody. What happened to me could happen to anyone, to the very good, to the less good, to those who know nothing and even to those who think they know everything; it could happen to you tomorrow, perhaps even tonight — one day, surely.

NIKOLAI BERDYAEV had a fine mind; indeed, his brain was so overloaded with ideas that his tongue sometimes stumbled. Since those days I have learned to admire him, but then he had, so far as I was concerned, one very grave weakness: he believed in God and, moreover, he did not write about him as one writes about a scientific hypothesis, which I regarded as permissible. No, he wrote about God as though he really existed, which I considered required proof. To fall back on a god to explain the world and its history seemed to me to be a piece of sophistry quite unworthy of a philosopher. A detective story in which the classic puzzle of solving a murder which has been committed in a locked room is resolved by the activity of a supernatural being capable of passing through walls wouldn't be worth much. Those were the kind of arguments I used at the time and that is why Berdyaev's *Un Nouveau Moyen Age* made absolutely no impression on me. This author was a believer; the conclusions he reached about Marxism, the Russian Revolution and the French Revolution stemmed from his beliefs; they were no concern of mine and made no impact on me.

This is more or less what I said to Willemin when he asked me to explain my remark that there was nothing to discuss about the book. Since the author believed in

God, everything he wrote followed on logically; between him and me no discussion was possible.

*

Willemin misunderstood me; he believed that Berdyaev had convinced me and thought we should celebrate the occasion by dining together. I was always happy to dine with him; I enjoyed his company, his lively mind, his talent for the flute, for medicine, for journalism, for cooking *à la lorraine*, for mimicry. I might not share his ideas but I often shared his jokes.

Not being fond of coming out into the open, and not wishing to spoil his evening, I decided not to explain my position to him; I'd leave him his illusory happiness, at least until dinner-time, perhaps until the dessert. This was the misunderstanding which, as I have already mentioned, played a part in my conversion.

*

The office having just closed, we set off in Willemin's old car (any sort of car was an unbelievable luxury in our world), hanging on to the doors to keep them from flying open. We crossed the Seine and went away from the Île Saint-Louis – evidently we were not going to Willemin's apartment.

When we reached the Place Maubert I assumed that we were heading for the Rue Mouffetard where we usually bought our fried fish in its newspaper wrapping. We should, I foresaw, eat under the bridges and that would be quite pleasant. We should pay one franc for the fish and a few pence for the bottle of wine which would be dark blue at the bottom and pleasantly mauve and translucent at the neck. When, however, we passed the turning to the Rue Mouffetard and did not take it I was left without a clue as to where we were bound for. Perhaps we would go to a restaurant though the hour was rather early.

(Too many details and too trivial, complains the reader, but he must allow for the fact that one is apt to go in for detail if one has had the strange experience of attending one's own birth.)

I asked no questions, I was happy to let my friend choose the way, but our journey became even less understandable as we drove in a circle round the Latin Quarter, turned back on our course and reached the Rue d'Ulm. What could be bringing us to this students' quarter, at present uninhabited on account of the holidays? We stopped, shortly after passing the École Normale Supérieure, in front of my old haunt, the École des Arts Décoratifs. Willemin got out and suggested that either I come along with him or wait for him for a few minutes in the car. I waited. No doubt he was going to call on someone. I watched him cross the road and push open a little door which stood near to a great iron gate above which I could see the steeple of a chapel.

Obviously he was going to pray, perhaps go to confession, certainly engage in one of those activities which take up so much of a Christian's time. All the more reason for me to stay in the car.

I⊤ was the eighth of July. The summer was glorious.
Straight in front of me the Rue d'Ulm, looking like a
sun-drenched trench, led off in the direction of the
Pantheon, which could be seen at its end. What thoughts
crossed my mind? I don't remember. No doubt, as usual,
they floated around looking vaguely for a ledge, an
angle, for some geometrical motif to rest on. As to my
inner life? So far as my conscience was concerned, it was
at peace, that is to say I was not suffering from any
disturbance, such as people say predispose one to mystical
experiences.

*

I had no heart-break. That very evening I had a rendez-
vous with a German girl at the Beaux-Arts; she had the
fine features which sometimes go with plumpness and
gave me the impression she would not defend her frontiers
very vigorously. (I mention this for the benefit of those
who explain religion by its opposite, who explain the
mind by the body, the greater by the less, and what's on
top by what's below.) Anyway, very soon the German
girl had so completely vanished from my mind that I
even forgot to put her off.

I was without any metaphysical problems. The last
time I had had any trouble of the sort had been at the age

of fifteen, as I have described earlier. Then it had seemed to me that the world by which I was besieged and deafened, the world which was so dumbly voluble, was about to hand me the key to its hieroglyphs, the secret of its being (and that this was imminent). But, the world did not reveal anything to me and since that time I had not tried to discover its secret.

Together with my socialist friends, I held that the world could be explained by politics plus history, and that metaphysics were the most disappointing of all pastimes. And certainly if I were to have imagined that there was a truth, the priests would have been the last people to whom I would have gone to learn about it and the Church (about which I had heard only in terms of some of her temporal malpractices) would have been quite the last place to which I would have gone to look for it.

My profession as a journalist had done nothing to diminish my scepticism though it had done a lot to quieten the anxieties which my disappointing youth had caused my parents. I was exercising my skill at too young an age, and had done so for too short a time, for my career to have brought me any of those disappointments which create a vacuum inside one and that sense of isolation which could favour the birth of an impulse towards religion. I had no worries. I was not a worry to anyone. Willemin's friendship had had the effect of withdrawing me from some undesirable relationships which I had formed in the past. The year had been calm, there had been no national emergencies and France was not under any immediate external threat; the alarm had not yet been sounded. I had no fixations. My health was good and I was very happy in so far as I was aware; the evening promised to be a pleasant one. I waited.

I had no curiosity about things relating to religion, for religion seemed to me to belong to another age.

*

It is now ten minutes past five. In two minutes' time I shall be a Christian.

A COMPLACENT atheist, I suspected nothing when, bored by waiting while Willemin was busy with his devotions, which were keeping him longer than he had expected, I pushed my way past the little gate to have a look at the building into which he had disappeared. My interest in it was that of a lover of architecture or perhaps that of a tourist.

*

What I had been able to see of the chapel over the gate was not very prepossessing and the Sisters will I hope forgive me if I say that when wholly disclosed to my view it did not prove any handsomer. It stood at the end of a small courtyard and had been built in a nineteenth-century English Neo-Gothic style, which, when it tidies up the original Gothic, petrifies it and deprives it of all movement. I am not writing this stricture to enjoy the dubious pleasure of criticizing a style that has now come to be admired but to make the point that no rush of artistic emotion had anything to do with what follows.

The inside is no more stimulating than the exterior. It is the banal careening of a stone ship whose dark grey lines stop and start before they have been given the chance to make the Cistercian encounter between austerity and beauty. The nave is divided into three distinct sections. In the first, near the entrance, the faithful pray in semi-darkness. Stained-glass windows, dimmed by neighbouring buildings, let in a little weak light which falls on various statues and there is a side altar covered with bouquets of flowers.

The second section is used by the nuns; their heads covered by black veils, they look like rows of well-behaved birds perched in bays of varnished wood. Later I was to learn that they belong to the order of 'L'Adoration Réparatrice' founded after the war of 1870 as a pious reparation for some excesses that took place during the Commune. They are not very numerous (this fact will be seen later to be important). They are a contemplative order; they have chosen to shut themselves up to give us freedom and to live in obscurity to give us light. According to materialistic standards – and for the following two minutes they were those to which I still subscribed – these women were totally useless.

They were chanting some sort of prayer, two choirs replying to each other from either side of the nave. The chant culminated at regular intervals in the exclamation: *gloria patri et filio, et spiritui sancto*, after which the two-part chant continued peacefully on its way. I had no idea that it was the psalms that were being sung or that I was attending matins. I was lulled by the swell of the canonical hours.

The end of the chapel was rather brightly lit. The high altar was draped in white and covered with a great many plants and candelabra and a variety of ornaments. Above it hung a large metal cross; at its centre there was a white disc, and three others that were slightly different were fixed to the extremities of the cross.

In the interest of art, I had previously visited churches

but I had never before seen a host, much less a monstrance with a host in it. I was therefore quite unaware that before me was the Blessed Sacrament below which many candles were burning. The other discs, the complicated gilt ornaments, all contributed to making identification of this distant sun still more difficult.

*

I didn't see the point of all this, naturally, since I was not looking for it. Standing by the door, I looked out for my friend, but I was not able to identify him among the kneeling figures. My glance went from the dimness to the light, fell on the congregation, travelled from the faithful to the nuns, and from the nuns to the altar without any thought consciously crossing my mind. Then, for no particular reason, I fixed my eyes on the second candle on the left-hand side of the cross.

It was at this moment that, suddenly, the series of extraordinary events was set in motion whose extreme violence was about to dismantle the absurd creature that I had been until that moment and give birth to the dazzled child I had never been.

FIRST, were the words: *spiritual life*.

They were not said to me nor did I form them in my mind; it was as though they were being spoken by someone close to me who was seeing something which I had not yet seen.

*

The last syllable had hardly brushed my conscious mind when an avalanche descended upon me. I am not saying that the heavens opened; they didn't open – they were hurled at me, they rose suddenly flashing silently from the depths of this innocent chapel in which they were mysteriously present.

How can I describe what took place in words which refuse to carry the sense, which indeed do worse, for they threaten to intercept what I have to say and in doing so to relegate my meaning to the land of fancy? Were a painter to be given the gift of seeing colours that are unknown to man what would he use to paint them with?

What can I say to describe that which I apprehended?

It was an indestructible crystal, totally transparent, luminous (to such a degree that any further intensity would have destroyed me), with a colour near to blue; a different world, whose brilliance and density made our world seem like the wraith of an unfulfilled dream. What I saw was reality; this was truth and I was seeing it from the dim shore on which I still stood. Now I knew that there is order in the universe and at its beginning, beyond the shining mists, the manifestation of God: a manifestation which is a presence, which is a person, the person whose existence I should have denied a moment ago, the presence of him whom the Christians call *Our Father*. And I knew that he was gentle, that his gentleness was unparalleled and that his was not the passive quality that is sometimes called by the name of gentleness, but an active shattering gentleness, far outstripping violence, able to smash the hardest stone and to smash something often harder than stone, the human heart.

*

This surging, overwhelming invasion brought with it a sense of joy comparable to that of a drowning man who is rescued at the last moment, but with this difference that it was at the moment in which I was being hauled to safety that I became aware of the mud in which, without noticing it, I had till then been stuck; and now I wondered how I had ever been able to breathe and to live in it.

*

The Church had become a new family to me. Now it was its business to guide me along the path I should take, for, in spite of appearances, I still had some way to go and this distance could not be miraculously shortened.

*

All these impressions which I find it so hard to translate into the deficient language of ideas and images occurred simultaneously and were so telescoped the one into the other that after many years I have not yet been able to digest all they contained. Everything was dominated by the presence, beyond and through the great assembly, of him before whom I had the joy of appearing as a child who had been forgiven and who had woken up to discover that everything is a gift.

It was fine outside. I was five years old and the world that once consisted of stone and pitch was now a great garden in which I would be allowed to play for so long as it pleased Heaven to leave me in the land of the living.

Willemin as he walked beside me seemed to sense something peculiar about my expression and observed me with clinical attention.

'What's come over you?' he enquired.

'I'm a Catholic.' And for good measure I added, 'Roman and Apostolic.'

'Your eyes are goggling.'

'God exists. It's all true.'

'If you could only see yourself.'

But I couldn't see myself; I was like an owl who has flown into the midday sun.

*

Five minutes later, on the terrace of a café in the Place Saint-André-des-Arts, I was telling Willemin all about it. At least all that, faced with the inexpressible, I was able to say of this world that had suddenly been spread out before me, all I could describe of that shining boulder which had silently destroyed the habitation of my childhood and made my surroundings vanish like mist. Around me the debris of my mental scaffolding littered the ground. I looked at the passers-by, who saw nothing, and I thought of the wonder they would feel if they were to experience the confrontation which had just been mine. I was certain that sooner or later this would happen to all of them and I rejoiced at the thought of the surprise of the unbelievers and of the doubters who were not even aware of their doubts.

God existed; he was here present, revealed and at the same time hidden by the light which, using neither speech nor images, conveyed a knowledge and a love of all things.

I realize that remarks such as these must appear extravagant, but what else am I to say if Christianity is true, if there is a truth, if the truth is a person who does not wish to be unknowable?

The miracle lasted for a month. Every morning I was delighted once again to experience that light which made daylight seem pale and that gentleness which I shall never forget and which is all that I know of theology.

Why I had to go on living on this planet when all this heavenly kingdom was so near at hand was not obvious to me but out of gratitude rather than understanding I accepted the situation.

However, each day the illumination and the gentleness lost a part of their intensity. Finally they vanished. But I was not left lonely. Truth would come to me in other modes; I would have to search for what I had almost found. A priest belonging to the order of the Holy Ghost undertook to prepare me for baptism by telling me about religion, of which, as will have been obvious, I had not the smallest knowledge.

What he described as Christian doctrine proved to be what I expected and I rejoiced in it. The teaching of the

Church was true and I took pleasure in all its details. The only fact that surprised me was that of the Eucharist. It seemed unbelievable. I was amazed that the love of God should have used such an astonishing means of communication and that for it bread, the food of the poor and of small children, had been God's choice.

Of all the gifts which Christianity was showering upon me, the Eucharist seemed to me the greatest.

OVERWHELMED with blessings, I anticipated that the rest of my life was going to be a sort of unending Christmas.

Experienced people to whom I spoke warned me that this privileged state was not going to last forever, that the laws of spiritual growth were the same for everyone, that, after the joy of the green pastures of experienced grace, I should be faced by the rock, the climb, the risks involved, that I was not always going to be a happy child. I did not listen to them. I was determined not to grow up a second time. Such was my wisdom, less wise than theirs.

They were right and I was wrong. Once the Christmas season had passed I had to face the stone and the tar and the things of a world which was slowly and cunningly returning to its old consistency. I lived a Good Friday and a Holy Saturday, lived them in a silence pierced only by a cry of anguish.

*

Twice the greatest suffering which can come upon a human being struck my home. Any parent will understand my meaning without requiring me to be more explicit. Twice I went to the cemetery, trying to discover the encompassing mercy behind the horror. Unable to revolt, incapable of taking refuge in doubt – for whom could I doubt except myself? – I lived with this sword piercing my heart, all the while knowing that God is love.

*

I am not writing this for the sake of completing my story, but it is a necessary part of my witness. One day I went to look at the place where some day I shall be buried. Out of curiosity I glanced to see who were my neighbours. I found this was the burial plot of the Sisters of L'Adoration Réparatrice. I know too well how these coincidences can be regarded either as a sign or rejected as a superstition. But the coincidence is enough for me.

The little Sisters who, five hundred kilometres away, were present at my birth will also be present at the hour of my death and I think, I believe, I know, that these two moments will be identical, will be one; material things will disappear and gentleness will return.

*

Love, to speak of you, eternity itself will be too brief.